TRIVIA CHOICE

TRIVIA CHOICE

MAUREEN & ALAN HIRON
& DAVID ELIAS

This first world edition published in Great Britain by
SEVERN HOUSE PUBLISHERS LTD of
4 Brook Street, London W1Y 1AA

Copyright © Maureen Hiron, Alan Hiron and David Elias

British Library Cataloguing in Publication Data
Hiron, Maureen
Trivia choice.
1. Questions and answers
I. Title II Hiron, Alan III. Elias, David
793.73 AG195

ISBN 0-7278-2099-0
ISBN 0-7278-2064-8 Pbk

All rights reserved. Unauthorised duplication contravenes applicable laws.

Phototypeset by The Word Factory, Rawtenstall, Lancs, England
Printed and bound in Great Britain by Anchor Brendon Ltd, Tiptree Essex

THE AUTHORS

Maureen Hiron and David Elias originally met when working together as consultants on Granada TV's Krypton Factor and as they never actually came to blows during production meetings, this seemed a good omen for their working together on other projects.

All three have an academic background, and David is a senior lecturer in English at Nottingham's Trent Polytechnic.

Maureen used to be the Head of the P E Department at a tough ILEA comprehensive school until her teaching career (and nearly Maureen) came to an abrupt end when a heavy metal fan extractor in the old school building parted company with its moorings and landed on her head.

Alan is the editor of Bridge International, 'Headmaster' of the London School of Bridge and a computer consultant, having been one of the very first into this then infant field.

If you stay to watch the credits at the end of quiz programmes on TV, chances are that you will see the name of David Elias, as he tends to be the first person whose phone rings when TV producers need question-setters and consultants.

Initially David was a very successful competitor on many TV and radio quiz shows – and has the prizes to prove it! After reaching the finals of 'Krypton Factor' in 1980 he was wooed to the other side of the cameras. Although he still makes the occasional appearance in the 'hot seat' he is barred from taking part in many shows, simply because he set the questions.

Maureen and Alan Hiron are perhaps best known as games inventors – Maureen's first-born, Continuo, became Britain's best-selling game within six weeks of first going on sale in 1982, and is now sold worldwide.

One of their next creations was the trivia game Quizwrangle – Britain's first. The natural follow-up to this was 'The Ultimate Trivia Quiz Game Book', with over 10 000 questions to Quizwrangle, which became a best-seller.

Maureen and Alan Hiron were the subjects of the 1985 BBC TV programme 'A Will to Win' and both have played Bridge for England and Britain.

INTRODUCTION

The craze for trivia is spreading fast. Radio, TV, pubs and clubs all run their own competitions. We've even been told of postal trivia gaming. But what is it that turns a general knowledge quiz into a so-called trivia quiz? The key is that the answer to any question is usually pretty useless. It may be bizarre, immediately forgotten, remembered for life . . . But it is rarely earth-shattering information. Will it affect your life to learn that Arthur Ransome, the author of best-selling children's books (*'Swallows and Amazons'*, *'Coot Club'* etc.) married Trotsky's secretary? We doubt it very much. However, what a curious snippet of *utterly* useless information!

Did you know that an angekkok is an Eskimo conjurer? We don't think that many of you will ever meet one and if you turn the conversation in such a way that your knowledge will be shown, how do you go about it? You can't just say, 'I see that Manchester United won again today. Which reminds me, do you know the word for an Eskimo conjurer?' People will think that you are potty and start avoiding you. . . .

For this book we have decided on a different format from just straight question and answer. Even if you haven't the slightest clue in which year vacuum cleaners were invented (or whether it was J Edgar Hoover or not) you are always offered four plausible, or zany-sounding alternatives.

Take care! Don't regard this as a work of reference! If one

of the alternatives is, say, 'The Russian Count who attempted to seduce Queen Victoria before her marriage' then, if the answer is wrong (and we sincerely hope it is), don't start repeating the libel. And some of the possible answers are completely outrageous.

At the very worst, you have a one in four chance. An even more entertaining thought is, if you are really reduced to guesswork, can you get inside the minds of the question-setters? Is it the obvious answer, is it one that seems reasonably likely, or is it the one that seems downright lunatic? We like to think that there has been a little bit of variety in the way that they have been shared out. And there are some out-and-out traps dotted about to keep you on your toes.

Bluff or double bluff? Come back to the vacuum cleaner. Was it really invented by J Edgar Hoover in 1929, by an unknown Russian inventor in 1926, by Mr 'Electrolux' Brown (as he became known) in 1921, or by J Murray Spangler in 1908? Well, we know the answer, but you will have to read on in order to find out.

PLAYING WITH TRIVIA

If you have a large number of questions, it is not difficult to organise a game, either between two individuals or two teams of any number.

However, with the four suggested answers to each question, there is even more scope. Work out your variations, but here is one thought.

With four or more players, 'A' asks the question to 'B'. Correct? Three points. Incorrect? The question passes to 'C' who now has only three alternatives left. Correct? Two points. Incorrect? Then on to 'D' who now has only two choices left and can only score one point.

As you can guess, the questioner then becomes 'B' and it is now 'C' who has the first choice. Everything goes clockwise, and you can arrange to play a set of number of complete circuits before you start. (Otherwise the temporary leader will look at his watch and say, 'Goodness me, 1.45am. My wife will probably be missing me – I must be off. I see that I am the winner . . .') Obviously you keep a score, but this shouldn't tax anyone's arithmetic – using the pegs on a cribbage board is very convenient if you can't find a pen.

TRIVIA CHOICE

1 Which newspaper was nicknamed 'The Thunderer'?
A. The Times B. News Chronicle
C. News of the World D. Daily Mirror

2 Which of the following virtuoso instrumentalists is a cellist?
A. Claudio Arrau B. Paul Tortellier
C. Rodney Friend D. Alfredo Campoli

3 Whose lace panties caused quite a stir at the Wimbledon Tennis Championships of 1949?
A. Helen Wills-Moody B. Suzanne Lenglen
C. Yvonne Goolagong D. Gussie Moran

4 Who was in command of the German Navy from 1914 –1916?
A. Admiral Donitz B. Baron Graf-Spee
C. Count Zeppelin D. Admiral Tirpitz

5 Which comic strip first appeared on October 2, 1950?
A. Garfield B. Peanuts
C. Andy Capp D. The Tramps

6 What is unique about the Basenji breed of dog?
A. It is hairless
B. It has one brown and one blue eye
C. It has no bark
D. It has disproportionately long legs

7 Name the two rival gangs in 'West Side Story'.
A. Ravens and Bulls

B. Cheetahs and Sharks
C. Sharks and Jets
D. Jets and Bulls

8 Why was policeman Trevor Lock awarded the George Medal?
A. Because of his actions following the Harrods bombing
B. For his action during the Iranian Embassy siege of 1980
C. For rescuing a complete family from a blazing house in Southall, the fire having been started by petrol being poured through the letter box, then set alight
D. For rescuing two boys who had fallen through thin ice while skating

9 In 1959, the first new theatre for 300 years was opened in the City of London. What was it called?
A. Windmill B. New Vic C. Garrick D. Mermaid

10 Who, according to Julius Caesar, had 'a lean and hungry look'?
A. Brutus B. Casca C. Cassius D. Marcellus

11 Which British pilot flew legless during World War Two?
A. Anthony Herbert B. Douglas Bader
C. William Donovan D. Audie Murphy

12 Having been delighted with Lewis Carroll's 'Alice in Wonderland', Queen Victoria asked him to send her a copy of his very next book. Why was she not amused?
A. Because his next book was a learned mathematical treatise, which he duly sent her
B. Because his next book was distinctly pornographic
C. His next book was a history of the St Leger race, in which Queen Victoria had zero interest
D. Because he forgot his promise to autograph it for her

ANSWERS pages 10–11: 1–A. 2.–B. 3–D. 4–D. 5–B. 6–C. 7–C. 8–B. 9–D. 10–C. 11–B. 12–A.

---

13 To which fish family does the trout belong?
A. Salmon B. Herring C. Shark D. Ray

14 Ole Bull of Norway was a virtuoso on which instrument?
A. Piano B. Violin C. Flute D. Trumpet

15 Ten years after the end of the Vietnam war, which is the last American outpost in Indo-China?
A. Tibet B. Thailand C. Nepal D. Afghanistan

16 Marking the death of Alfred Nobel, on which day of the year are Nobel Prizes traditionally presented?
A. January 20 B. July 8
C. September 18 D. November 10

17 'I knew if I stayed around long enough, something like this would happen.' Which writer wanted this as his epitaph?
A. Oscar Wilde B. George Bernard Shaw
C. George Orwell D. Ernest Hemingway

18 Benedictine is named after the Benedictine monks who invented it. What other famous drink was invented by a Benedictine monk?
A. Sloe gin
B. Bourbon whisky
C. The first real, sparkling champagne
D. Calvados brandy

19 Who was the star of the ITMA radio programmes?
A. Tony Hancock B. Sid James
C. Tommy Handley D. Jimmy Edwards

20 The famous Winston Churchill speech of 1940, 'We shall fight on the beaches', was actually delivered by whom?
A. Winston Churchill himself
B. Actor Norman Stanley
C. Clement Attlee
D. John Gielgud

21 Who directed and starred in the film 'Yentl'?
A. Omar Sharif B. Topol
C. Barbra Streisand D. David Niven

22 What is the checkpoint between East and West Berlin?
A. Charlie B. Freddie C. Bertie D. Benny

23 In 1884 what caused the death of Allan Pinkerton, the founder of the US detective agency?
A. He accidentally bit his tongue and died of the resultant gangrene
B. He was killed by one of his own operatives, who mistook him for a wanted gunman as he had omitted to tell his men that he would be present at the showdown
C. He was run over by one of the first cars on the roads of New York
D. He was the victim of a revenge killing.

24 'You can lead a horticulture, but you can't make her think', was the result of a challenge to a well-known wit to create a saying using the word 'horticulture'. Who was it?
A. Mark Twain B. W C Fields
C. Oscar Wilde D. Dorothy Parker

25 What was the first ever message sent by telegraph by its inventor, Samuel Morse?
A. 'Send 100 dollars quickly'
B. 'What hath God wrought?'
C. 'Come quickly, I need you'
D. 'Will you have dinner with me tonight?'

ANSWERS pages 12–13: 13–A. 14–B. 15–B. 16–D. 17–B. 18–C. 19–C. 20–B. 21–C. 22–A. 23–A. 24–D. 25–B.

---

26 Dick Francis is now best known as a writer of thrillers. What was his previous profession?
A. Solicitor B. Flat race jockey
C. Chauffeur D. Steeplechase jockey

27 Who succeeded Walter Winterbottom as manager of England's soccer team?
A. Matt Busby B. Alf Ramsey
C. Don Revie D. Brian Clough

28 Composing the music for 'Pack Up Your Troubles in Your Old Kit Bag and Smile, Smile, Smile' won first prize for Sergeant Felix Powell during World War One. For what was the competition held?
A. The best tune to the words of the lyricist, George Asaf
B. The most apt song for in-step marching
C. The best morale-building song for the armed forces
D. A suitable song as a forces National Anthem

29 The flower Goat's-beard has another curious name. What is it?
A. The Marsh Mallow plant B. Black Bryony
C. Old Man's Beard D. Jack-go-to-bed-at-noon

30 Which journalist wrote the book about the activities of the Secret Service, 'Too Secret Too Long'?
A. Brian Walden B. Shaun Usher
C. William Hickey D. Chapman Pincher

31 What is a lipogram?

A. An imprint of the lips, as an alternative to fingerprints
B. A work written omitting one particular letter of the alphabet
C. The American version of Kissograms
D. A blueprint from which bottle tops and jars are made

32 Franklin D Roosevelt was elected President of the United States four times. From what handicap did he suffer?
A. His legs were paralysed by polio
B. He had only two fingers on his right hand
C. He had a club foot
D. He was blind in one eye

33 In which year did Switzerland first allow women to vote?
A. 1906 B. 1919 C. 1945 D. 1971

34 A British firm exports in excess of £50 000 worth of petrol to the Arabs each year. How come?
A. As part of an OPEC agreement
B. In exchange for a special type of sand
C. In the form of lighter fuel
D. Of course they don't

35 For how much were Fred Astaire's legs insured?
A. 100 000 dollars B. 350 000 dollars
C. 650 000 dollars D. 1 000 000 dollars

36 Which is the eighteenth book of the Old Testament?
A. Psalms B. Isaiah C. Job D. Deuteronomy

37 In which part of the body is a bone called the cochlea?
A. Hands B. Feet C. Inner ear D. Lower back

38 Who said, 'I am free of all prejudices. I hate everyone equally'?
A. Oscar Wilde B. The Yorkshire Ripper
C. W C Fields D. Jack Benny

ANSWERS pages 14–15: 26–D. 27–B. 28–C. 29–D. 30–D. 31–B. 32–A. 33–D. 34–C. 35–C. 36–C. 37–C. 38–C.

---

39 Name Oliver Goldsmith's deserted village.
A. Brunette B. Blond C. Auburn D. Redhead

40 Cars from which country carry the international registration sign CH?
A. Czechoslovakia B. Holland
C. Austria D. Switzerland

41 What are 'Iron Goddess of Mercy', 'Old Man's Eyebrows' and 'Hairy Crab'?
A. Wild flowers B. Chinese teas
C. Fishing flies D. Tropical cacti

42 Anthony Hopkins has broadcast on the radio for over 30 years. On which subject?
A. Astrology B. Politics C. America D. Music

43 Who wrote the ballet 'Coppelia'?
A. Debussy B. Delibes C. Dvorak D. Donizetti

44 Which wife of Henry VIII had her heart stolen? (After she was dead.)
A. Anne of Cleves B. Catherine Parr
C. Anne Boleyn D. Catherine Howard

45 Shawls copied from Indian originals made which place in Scotland famous?
A. Paisley B. Hawick C. Perth D. Aberdeen

46 On which island is 'The Teahouse of the August Moon' set?

A. Okinawa B. Nagasaki C. Hong Kong D. Hawaii

47 In its powdered state, what colour is caffeine?
A. Black B. Brown C. White D. Yellow

48 The annual Three Choirs Festival is held in rotation at Worcester, Gloucester and which other cathedral city?
A. Hereford B. Leicester
C. Manchester D. Llandudno

49 How many tricks are needed for a small slam at bridge?
A. 9 B. 10 C. 11 D. 12

50 Which author, now famous in his own right, co-authored Malcolm X's autobiography?
A. Alex Haley B. John Steinbeck
C. Jack London D. Alvin Moscow

51 What are variously referred to as 'inert', 'rare' and 'noble'?
A. Gases B. Cacti
C. Swordfish D. Hereditary earldoms

52 Which Ivy League university is at New Haven, Connecticut?
A. Yale B. Harvard C. Princeton D. Columbus

53 How many play on a regular field hockey team?
A. 5 B. 7 C. 9 D. 11

54 On average, how many hours sleep did Napoleon Bonaparte have in each 24?
A. Between 3 and 4 B. Between 5 and 6
C. Between 7 and 8 D. Between 9 and 10

55 Which game do the Tampa Bay Rowdies play?
A. American Football B. Baseball
C. Basketball D. Soccer

ANSWERS pages 16–17: 39–C. 40–D. 41–B. 42–D. 43–B. 44–C. 45–A. 46–A. 47–C. 48–A. 49–D. 50–A. 51–A. 52–A. 53–D. 54–A. 55–D.

---

56 Anne Boleyn possessed what physical deviation(s) from the norm?
A. 12 toes
B. 12 fingers
C. 11 fingers and 3 breasts
D. 12 toes, 11 fingers and 3 breasts

57 For which city was the well-known dandy Beau Nash Master of Ceremonies in the 18th century?
A. Cheltenham B. Edinburgh
C. Leamington Spa D. Bath

58 Which first was Alan Whitehead's?
A. He was the very first contender on the very first 'Mastermind'
B. He was the first person to 'break the bank' at Monte Carlo
C. He was the first person whose occupation was not guessed by the panel on 'What's My Line'
D. He was the first civilian to refuse to accept an MBE

59 Whose band made the first jazz tour of Russia, in 1962?
A. Duke Ellington's B. Benny Goodman's
C. Count Basie's D. Oscar Peterson's

60 From which country did the 1981 Miss World, Pilin Leon, come?
A. Argentina B. Jamaica C. Venezuela D. USA

61 By what name is the wine Egri Bikaver more familiarly known?

A. Bull's Blood B. Retsina
C. Asti Spumante D. Metaxa

62 In which work does Lady Dulcinea de Tobosa feature?
A. Don Quixote B. Lady Windermere's Fan
C. She Stoops to Conquer D. As You Like It

63 Which book had the original title, 'The Sea Cook'?
A. Robinson Crusoe B. Kidnapped
C. Mr Midshipman Easy D. Treasure Island

64 What is the monetary unit of Mexico?
A. Peseta B. American dollar C. Peso D. Dinar

65 How did Gyles Brandreth rewrite Shakespeare's 'Hamlet'?
A. By omitting the letter 'I' throughout – changing the wording wherever necessary so that it still makes sense
B. As a new work entitled 'Rosenkrantz and Guildenstern Are Dead'
C. By making Polonius the central character
D. By reversing the sexes of the original characters

66 When the dove returned to Noah's Ark with a leaf, what kind of leaf was it?
A. Fig B. Palm C. Olive D. Cedar

67 In P C Wren's 'Beau Geste' the plot centred on a precious stone named 'The Blue Water'. What type of gem is this?
A. Diamond B. Ruby C. Emerald D. Sapphire

68 On the Soviet Union flag, three objects are depicted. A hammer and a sickle are two of them – what is the third?
A. A hand B. A star C. An eagle D. A small sun

69 What is the capital of South Africa?
A. Pretoria B. Durban
C. Johannesburg D. Port Elizabeth

ANSWERS pages 18–19: 56–C. 57–D. 58–A. 59–B. 60–C. 61–A. 62–A. 63–D. 64–C. 65–A. 66–C. 67–D. 68–B. 69–A.

---

70 According to legend, who will return to save England from disaster at some time in the future?
A. St George B. King Arthur
C. William the Conqueror D. Brian Clough

71 Curiously enough, the first ever international cricket match was played between Canada and the USA – countries not normally noted for their prowess at this game. In which year did it take place?
A. 1824 B. 1844 C. 1864 D. 1884

72 What is the distinguishing flavour of the liqueur Crème de Cassis?
A. Strawberry B. Blackcurrant C. Mint D. Coconut

73 Kelper is the name given to people born in which islands?
A. Shetlands B. Falklands C. Orkneys D. Leeward

74 Who was imprisoned for the crime committed by Major Marie Charles Esterhazy?
A. Alfred Dreyfus B. James Montgomery
C. Julius and Ethel Rosenberg D. Alger Hiss

75 How long did it take Robert Louis Stevenson to write 'The Strange Case of Dr Jekyll and Mr Hyde'?
A. Three days B. Three weeks
C. Three months D. Three years

76 Who is the host of TV's 'Blockbusters'?
A. Robert Robinson B. Bob Holness

C. Gordon Burns D. Bamber Gascoigne

77 Which was the first country to introduce old age pensions?
A. Great Britain B. Germany
C. Sweden D. New Zealand

78 What role does Katherine Helmond play in 'Soap'?
A. Jessica B. Mary
C. Eunice D. Lesley (Billy's amorous teacher)

79 Who sang (some say growled) 'Wand'rin Star' from the film 'Paint Your Wagon' which became a No 1 hit in 1970?
A. Lee Marvin B. Louis Armstrong
C. Eartha Kitt D. John Wayne

80 Who wrote the novels 'Hotel' and 'Airport'?
A. Harold Robbins B. Arthur Hailey
C. Frederick Forsyth D. Norman Mailer

81 Of which country is LOT the national airline?
A. Bulgaria B. Czechoslovakia
C. Poland D. Liechtenstein

82 What are the colours of the five interlocking rings of the Olympic flag?
A. Black, blue, green, red, yellow
B. Orange, blue, green, red, yellow
C. Black, orange, blue, green, red
D. Brown, orange, blue, green, red

83 Which is the second largest city to Paris in France?
A. Lyons B. Nice C. Marseilles D. Monaco

84 Which singer's backing group was the 'Blue Moon Boys'?
A. Frank Sinatra B. Elvis Presley
C. Carly Simon D. Jack Jones

Answers pages 20–21: 70–B. 71–B. 72–B. 73–B. 74–A. 75–A. 76–B. 77–B. 78–A. 79–A. 80–B. 81–C. 82–A. 83–C. 84–B.

---

85 Who won the 1970 World Showjumping Championships on Beethoven?
A. Harvey Smith B. Liz Edgar
C. David Broome D. Malcolm Pyrah

86 What was the first British car registration number?
A. A B. 1 C. A1 D. AAA111

87 In which year did the United States of America enter World War Two?
A. 1939 B. 1940 C. 1941 D. 1942

88 For which Beatles hit was 'Daisy Hawkins' the original working title?
A. Eleanor Rigby B. Yesterday
C. Love Me Do D. Yellow Submarine

89 What is a hummum?
A. A tea urn
B. A turkish bath
C. A musical instrument
D. A dress mainly worn in Haiti

90 Which British bank has Hiron the horse as its emblem?
A. Lloyds B. NatWest C. Midland D. Barclays

91 What is the family name of the Dukes of Wellington?
A. Wellesley B. Churchill
C. Spencer D. Marlborough

92 On a standard British typewriter keyboard which letter comes between 'X' and 'V'?
A. B B. C C. D D. E

93 What colour coat does the trap 1 greyhound always wear in the UK?
A. Red B. Blue C. White D. Black

94 During World War One, Robert Baden-Powell, the founder of the Scout movement, served in what capacity?
A. As an intelligence officer in the Navy
B. As a communications officer
C. As a spy
D. As a food and supplies co-ordinator

95 What is the Peter Principle?
A. 'In a hierarchy, every employee tends to rise to his level of incompetence'
B. 'Every action has an equal and opposite reaction'
C. 'If anything can go wrong, it will'
D. 'Please leave this room/office as you would wish to find it'

96 What did Hitler intend renaming Berlin after World War Two?
A. Victoria B. Hitlerplatz
C. Germanis D. Reichland

97 Which saint is associated with Assissi?
A. St Patrick B. St Christopher
C. St Francis D. St Germain

98 Which film producer was reputed to have said, 'Why only twelve apostles? Go out and get thousands'?
A. Orson Welles B. Steven Spielberg
C. Sam Goldwyn D. Lew Grade

ANSWERS pages 22–23: 85–C. 86–C. 87–C. 88–A. 89–B. 90–A. 91–A. 92–B. 93–A. 94–C. 95–A. 96–C. 97–C. 98–C.

---

99 The Gulf of Bothnia separates which two countries?
A. Sweden and Finland B. Sweden and Denmark
C. Finland and Iceland D. Sweden and Iceland

100 How many sheets of paper are in a ream?
A. 20 B. 100 C. 500 D. 1 000

101 How long after Mozart had finished writing his opera 'Don Giovanni' did its first performance take place?
A. One day B. One month C. One year D. 100 years

102 By what name is Joe Yule Junior better known?
A. James Garner B. Dean Martin
C. Mickey Rooney D. Jerry Lewis

103 Without looking at the front or back covers, who are the publishers of this book?
A. Penguin B. Faber C. Methuen D. Severn House

104 'Idomeneo' is a Mozart opera. But who was Idomeneo?
A. A Nubian slave B. A king of Crete
C. A Greek dignitary D. A Turkish ruler

105 What is Tommy Steele's real name?
A. Tommy Steel B. Tommy Green
C. Tommy Boyd D. Tommy Hicks

106 Evonne Goolagong (Cawley) won her second Wimbledon tennis singles championship how many years after winning her first?

A. 1 B. 5 C. 9 D. 11

107 Which was the last year in which real silver was used in British coins? (Apart from Maundy money, for which it is still used.)
A. 1932 B. 1939 C. 1946 D. 1953

108 How many countries competed in the first of the modern Olympic Games?
A. 9 B. 18 C. 27 D. 36

109 According to J R R Tolkein, their creator, what is the favourite food of Hobbits?
A. Apples B. Mushrooms C. Cabbages D. Lettuces

110 On which continent is Queen Maud Land?
A. North America B. Antarctica C. Africa D. Asia

111 What was the most popular feminine first name around the turn of the 20th century in England?
A. Ethel B. Gladys C. Mary D. Florence

112 How is Queen Elizabeth II related to Queen Victoria?
A. Great-great-great-granddaughter
B. Great-great-granddaughter
C. Great-granddaughter
D. Granddaughter

113 What does '2' represent on the Beaufort scale?
A. Slight breeze B. Light Air
C. Strong breeze D. Hurricane

114 Which country has the oldest national flag, dating from 1219?
A. Great Britain B. Iceland C. Denmark D. Greece

ANSWERS pages 24–25: 99–A. 100–C. 101–A. 102–C. 103–D. 104–B. 105–D. 106–C. 107–C. 108–A. 109–B. 110–B. 111–D. 112–B. 113–A. 114–C.

---

115 Which US President's wife used the CB handle 'First Mama'?
A. Nancy Reagan B. Pat Nixon
C. Betty Ford D. Varina Davis

116 Where were the 1984 Summer Olympic Games held?
A. Rome B. Mexico C. Melbourne D. Los Angeles

117 What was Jack Ketch's trade or profession during the 17th century?
A. Surgeon B. Hangman C. Judge D. Sheriff

118 Which mountain range separates France from Spain?
A. Andes B. Alps C. Himalayas D. Pyrenees

119 Who composed the opera 'Rigoletto'?
A. Puccini B. Wagner C. Rossini D. Verdi

120 Who portrayed Glenn Miller in the film 'The Glenn Miller Story'?
A. James Mason B. James Stewart
C. James Dean D. James Robertson Justice

121 At which sport has Peter Wheeler captained England?
A. Cricket B. Rugby Union
C. Golf D. Hang-gliding

122 What colour is the 8-ball in pool?
A. Black B. Red C. Blue D. White

123 Phoebe Anne Moses, also known as Annie Oakley was given the name of 'Little Miss Sureshot' by which Indian Chief?
A. Geronimo B. Crazy Horse
C. Sitting Bull D. Running Water

124 Who composed the piece 'Eine Kleine Nachtmusik'?
A. Bach B. Beethoven C. Haydn D. Mozart

125 From where to where were the headquarters of NATO moved in 1967?
A. Brussels to Paris B. Paris to Brussels
C. London to Paris D. London to Brussels

126 How many grams are in 1lb?
A. 258 B. 454 C. 767 D. 1 000

127 By what more colloquial name is the group of stars called the Pleiades better known?
A. The Seven Sisters B. Orion the Hunter
C. The Great Bear D. The Plough

128 Bizet's opera 'The Fair Maid of Perth' was based on a novel by which writer?
A. Scott Fitzgerald B. Sir Walter Scott
C. Walter de la Mare D. Mary Shelley

129 By what name was Jeanine Deckers, who had a massive hit in 1963 with 'Dominique', better known?
A. Lulu B. The Singing Nun
C. Dusty Springfield D. Carole King

130 For what is Thomas Telford best remembered?
A. Supporting the Tolpuddle Martyrs
B. Improving food technology
C. Opposing slavery
D. Building bridges and canals

ANSWERS pages 26–27: 115–C. 116–D. 117–B. 118–D. 119–D. 120–B. 121–B. 122–A. 123–C. 124–D. 125–B. 126–B. 127–A. 128–B. 129–B. 130–D.

---

131 Name the treaty of 1842 which officially ceded Hong Kong to Britain
A. Peking Treaty B. Nanking Treaty
C. Hong Kong Treaty D. Canton Treaty

132 Where on your body would you find your philtrum?
A. On your hands as it is the cuticle of your fingernail
B. On your face, as it is the central, grooved part of your upper lip
C. In your ear, as it is the tube leading from your inner ear into your throat
D. On your tummy – it's another name for the belly-button

133 Devonshire Park, Eastbourne, is an important centre for which sport?
A. Tennis B. Rugby C. Football D. Cricket

134 What does the musical direction *con sordino* mean?
A. With feeling B. Sweetly
C. With mute D. All together

135 Hugh Town is on which island(s) in the UK?
A. Shetland Isles B. Scilly Isles
C. Isle of Sheppey D. Isle of Wight

136 A large quantity of gold was recovered from a sunken British ship in 1981. What was the name of the ship?
A. HMS Carlisle B. HMS Newcastle
C. HMS Edinburgh D. HMS Sheffield

137 In which year did Umberto II, the last king of Italy, leave that country?
A. 1901 B. 1933 C. 1939 D. 1946

138 Which event does the film 'Tora! Tora! Tora!' encapsulate?
A. The Spanish Bullfighting Challenge of 1963
B. The annual running of the bulls through the streets
C. The attack on Pearl Harbour
D. The attempted Jumbo jet hijack of 1976

139 How many symphonies did Brahms compose?
A. 1 B. 4 C. 7 D. 10

140 What part did John Le Mesurier play in 'Dad's Army'?
A. Captain Mainwaring B. Sergeant Wilson
C. Corporal Jones D. Private Frazer

141 How many microns are in a centimetre?
A. 1 000 B. 10 000 C. 10 0000 D. 1 000 000

142 If it is 9.00pm Greenwich Mean Time in London, what is the time in Moscow?
A. Midnight B. 6.00am C. Midday D. 9.00am

143 Who recorded the LP, 'Tapestry'?
A. Joan Armatrading B. Michael Jackson
C. The Ronettes D. Carole King

144 'Looks Even Better on a Man' is the advertising slogan for which product?
A. Gloria Vanderbilt designer jeans B. Tootal Shirts
C. Stetson hats D. Rael-Brook Toplin Shirts

145 Which Prime Minister said, 'I'm an optimist. But I'm an optimist who takes his raincoat'?
A. Harold Wilson B. Clement Attlee
C. Harold Macmillan D. Edward Heath

ANSWERS pages 28–29: 131–B. 132–B. 133–A. 134–C. 135–B. 136–C. 137–D. 138–C. 139–B. 140–B. 141–B. 142–A. 143–D. 144–B. 145–A.

---

146 Which comedian introduced a character who repeatedly used the catchphrase 'Katanga'?
A. Lenny Bruce B. Lenny Henry
C. Lenny the Lion D. Jack Benny

147 Of which novel is Winston Smith the central character?
A. Fahrenheit 451 B. Portnoy's Complaint
C. The Last of the Mohicans D. 1984

148 Who was the first darts player ever to perform a 9-dart finish to a 501 start on TV?
A. John Lowe B. Eric Bristow
C. Leighton Rees D. Jocky Wilson

149 Where was the very first FA Cup Final played, in 1872?
A. White City B. Stamford Bridge
C. The Oval D. Highbury

150 Who first made what is now probably the most quoted remark in political journalism, 'A week is a long time in politics'?
A. Harold Macmillan B. Edward Heath
C. Harold Wilson D. William Gladstone

151 Which TV series has as its introductory phrase, 'To boldly go where no man has gone before' – now frequently parodied as, 'To split infinitives as no man has ever split them before'?
A. Star Trek B. Mork and Mindy
C. Batman D. A Hitchhiker's Guide to the Galaxy

152 Which vegetable is used to make up the dish 'Eggs Florentine'?
A. Cabbage B. Green Pepper
C. Broccoli D. Spinach

153 Who is the famous son of Naomi Cantor?
A. Irving Berlin B. Al Jolson
C. Eddie Cantor D. Abraham Lincoln

154 Which is the smallest instrument in the woodwind section of a symphony orchestra?
A. Flute B. Piccolo C. Oboe D. Clarinet

155 Which is the only letter of the alphabet not represented in the names of the fifty states of the USA?
A. Z B. J C. Q D. X

156 Which was the first country to have all births, marriages and deaths recorded?
A. Great Britain B. Sweden C. France D. Canada

157 In which subject has Margaret Thatcher gained a degree – not an honorary one?
A. Zoology B. Economics C. Chemistry D. Physics

158 What is Cliff Lazarenko's game?
A. Snooker B. Bowls C. Darts D. Chess

159 The film 'Psycho' was based upon whose writings?
A. Bram Stoker B. Mary Shelley
C. William Sloane D. Robert Bloch

160 What is, or was, a 'Collins'?
A. A rabbit punch to the neck
B. A hot drink, based on heavily spiced cider
C. A thank-you letter for hospitality
D. A small breed of dog, often owned by gypsies

ANSWERS pages 30–31: 146–B. 147–D. 148–A. 149–C. 150–C. 151–A. 152–D. 153–B. 154–B. 155–C. 156–D. 157–C. 158–C. 159–D. 160–C.

---

161 From whom or what do these words come? 'Is it a book that you would have lying around in your own house? Is this a book that you would even wish your wife or your servant to read?'
   A. The New York Times review of 'Portnoy's Complaint'
   B. The Washington Post's review of 'Lolita'
   C. The first ever printed review of Jane Austen's 'Pride and Prejudice'
   D. The prosecuting counsel at the 'Lady Chatterley's Lover' trial

162 By what name is the weekly publication 'The London Charivari' more familiarly known?
   A. Tit-bits   B. Punch   C. Cosmopolitan   D. Vogue

163 Who preceded Jehu as King of Israel?
   A. David   B. Solomon   C. Belshazzar   D. Ahab

164 Who were the first husband and wife team ever to be officially executed in the USA?
   A. Julius and Ethel Rosenberg – for treason
   B. Tom and Alice Manson – for cult murders
   C. Jack and Elizabeth Ruby – for assassination of a political figure
   D. No husband and wife team has been officially executed

165 Which is the chief gas in the earth's atmosphere?
   A. Hydrogen   B. Oxygen
   C. Carbon Dioxide   D. Nitrogen

166 Which British admiral lost a leg while pursuing French ships in the West Indies?
A. Benbow B. Nelson C. Hardy D. Hornblower

167 In which year was a woman last executed for witchcraft in England?
A. 1582 B. 1632 C. 1682 D. 1732

168 How many states were there when the United States of America was first united?
A. 7 B. 13 C. 27 D. 43

169 Which wedding anniversary is pearl?
A. 10th B. 20th C. 30th D. 40th

170 Which newspaper once published a single edition (Sunday) that weighed over 7 pounds?
A. Sunday Times B. New York Times
C. Observer D. Washington Post

171 What colour is the Golden Gate bridge?
A. Gold B. Orange C. Red D. White

172 Who was F W H Myers?
A. Founder of the Psychical Research Society
B. Founder of the British Rum Connoisseurs Society
C. Founder of the Helsinki Cricket Club
D. Founder of the British Darts Union

173 In snooker, how many points does potting a red ball, a blue ball, a red ball and a pink ball score?
A. 9 B. 11 C. 13 D. 15

174 Which sport is played in Yankee Stadium?
A. American Football B. Baseball
C. Ice Hockey D. Basketball

ANSWERS pages 32–33: 161–D. 162–B. 163–D. 164–A. 165–D. 166–A. 167–C. 168–B. 169–C. 170–B. 171–B. 172–A. 173–C. 174–B.

---

175 In music key signatures, which is always the first sharp?
A. F B. C C. G D. D

176 For what was Albert Freese celebrated?
A. In a first round at Wimbledon he led 6–0, 6–0, 5–0, 40–love and still lost
B. He was the first man to break the 4-hour barrier for the running backwards marathon
C. His First Division football career lasted only 10 seconds – then he was injured and never played again
D. He played hockey for the English national *ladies* team!

177 In which country did spaghetti, macaroni and the like originate?
A. Italy B. Greece C. China D. India

178 At what average speed was the very first Grand Prix motor race won, in 1901?
A. 26 mph B. 46 mph C. 66 mph D. 86 mph

179 When Elvis Presley first appeared on American TV's Ed Sullivan show, he was only screened from the waist up. Why was this?
A. Because it was considered that his hip gyrations would prove offensive and an outrage against public decency
B. Some obscure Union rules might have led to problems if he had been shown in full, wiggle and all
C. Because his lurex trousers did not conform to the then accepted dress code
D. His zipper had migrated downwards

180 Alexander Selkirk's experiences led to the creation of which fictional character?
A. Horatio Hornblower B. Tom Sawyer
C. David Copperfield D. Robinson Crusoe

181 'What A Lot I Got' was the advertising slogan for which product?
A. Lego B. Golden Wonder Salted Peanuts
C. Camay Soap D. Smarties

182 Who was the husband of Helen, whose kidnapping led to the Trojan War?
A. Paris B. Achilles C. Menelaus D. Priam

183 What is the common name for the sternum?
A. Breastbone B. Shoulderblade
C. Collar bone D. Rib cage

184 When is Lady Day?
A. January 25 B. March 25
C. June 25 D. September 25

185 Which animal is slang for £500?
A. Pony B. Monkey C. Hippo D. Tiger

186 What was Japan's Naomi Vemura's claim to fame in 1978?
A. He was the first Japanese to play English county cricket
B. He swam the English Channel in the nude
C. He fell off the Eiffel Tower, and lived
D. He was the first man to travel alone to the North Pole

187 Which country was the first to have a woman Member of Parliament?
A. New Zealand B. Great Britain
C. Greece D. Finland

ANSWERS pages 34–35: 175–A. 176–B. 177–C. 178–B. 179–A. 180–D. 181–D. 182–C. 183–A. 184–B. 185–B. 186–D. 187–D.

---

188 How old was William Pitt the Younger when he first became Prime Minister of Great Britain, having already refused the position the previous year?
A. 24 B. 29 C. 32 D. 41

189 Which mathematician was Member of Parliament for Cambridge in 1688?
A. Lewis Carroll B. John Donne
C. Jonathan Swift D. Isaac Newton

190 Where was Rudyard Kipling's poem 'If' first printed?
A. In an anthology of verse
B. In the obituary column of The Times
C. In the 'People' column of The News of the World
D. In Reader's Digest

191 Dungevan castle, on the Isle of Skye has been the home of the chiefs of which clan for over 600 years?
A. McLaren B. McLeod C. MacMillan D. Stewart

192 Which country worldwide has the lowest infant death rate?
A. USA B. UK C. Japan D. Sweden

193 How did Jerome Napoleon Bonaparte die, in 1945?
A. He was killed in action in Germany
B. He tripped over the lead of his wife's dog in Central Park, New York, and subsequently died from the injuries he sustained
C. He was killed in an aircrash when making a pilgrimage to Paris to visit the grave of his famous ancestor

D. He drowned while skating on thin ice, which gave way under him

194 Where was John Cleland when he wrote 'Fanny Hill'?
A. On an ocean cruise, trying to forget a broken romance
B. In exile
C. In Newgate Prison
D. Acting in a play, and having plenty of time between appearances on stage, as he only had a minor role

195 Who made famous the phrase, 'George, don't do that'?
A. Mrs Dale of diary fame B. Joyce Grenfell
C. Goldie Hawn D. Liz Fraser

196 Joan of Arc was burnt at the stake in 1431. In which year was she canonised?
A. 1432 B. 1631 C. 1840 D. 1920

197 Which planet did William Herschel discover in 1781?
A. Saturn B. Jupiter C. Uranus D. Pluto

198 How many eggs do hummingbirds lay in their lifetime?
A. 2 B. 20 C. 200 D. 2 000

199 By what name was Robert Stroud known?
A. The Hillbilly Cat B. Pinkertons Ace
C. The Birdman of Alcatraz D. The Boston Strangler

200 Which of the following was *not* one of the original 4 'Goons'?
A. Michael Bentine B. Peter Sellers
C. Spike Milligan D. Harry Secombe

201 By what name is Schubert's Eighth Symphony otherwise known?
A. Surprise B. Choral C. Great D. Unfinished

ANSWERS pages 36–37: 188–A. 189–D. 190–B. 191–B. 192–D. 193–B. 194–C. 195–B. 196–D. 197–C. 198–A. 199–C. 200–None of them: these *were* the original 4 Goons. 201–D.

---

202 Which comedian originated the use of the catchwords, 'Swinging' and 'Dodgy' in the 1960s?
A. Jack Benny B. Norman Vaughan
C. Tommy Trinder D. Al Read

203 Who was the original Mrs Dale in the long running radio series, 'Mrs Dale's Diary'?
A. Ellis Powell B. Hylda Baker
C. Ena Sharples D. Jessie Matthews

204 Is this line from Shakespeare's 'The Merchant of Venice' an accurate quotation? 'All that glitters is not gold.' If not, what should it be?
A. It's correct
B. 'All that glistens is not gold'
C. 'All that glisters is not gold'
D. 'All that sparkles is not gold'

205 In which country was soccer's first World Cup held?
A. Paraguay B. Brazil C. Chile D. Uruguay

206 Who is or was the famous son of Jeanette Jerome?
A. Richard Burton B. Max Wall
C. Winston Churchill D. Charlie Chaplin

207 What piece of nastiness did Gary Sobers perpetrate on bowler Malcolm Nash?
A. He hit 6 sixes off him in one over
B. He knocked him out while he was fielding at silly mid-on

C. He muddled up their kits and Nash wore the wrong trousers, which split embarrassingly during the match
D. He chased off a stray dog which then made straight for Nash and bit him

208 Who wrote 'Pudd'n-head Wilson'?
A. Mark Twain B. Richard Llewellyn
C. Robert Browning D. Robbie Burns

209 Of which great composer was Anna Maria Pertl the mother?
A. Brahms B. Mozart C. Haydn D. Handel

210 Which of the following novels was *not* written by Jane Austen?
A. Emma B. Pride and Prejudice
C. Wuthering Heights D. Northanger Abbey

211 What colour is a peacock's egg?
A. White B. Blue speckled
C. Brown D. Bluish-green

212 What was the arrow of gold of Joseph Conrad's novel of the same name?
A. An arrow B. A tiepin
C. A scarab beetle D. A hairpin

213 What was Captain Matthew Webb the first to do?
A. Go over Niagara Falls in a barrel, and survive
B. Swim the English Channel
C. Fly a helicopter commercially
D. Win an official spaghetti-eating contest

214 In Lewis Carroll's poem 'Jabberwocky' who or what is described as 'frumious'?
A. The Jabberwock B. The Borogoves
C. The Toves D. The Bandersnatch

ANSWERS pages 38–39: 202–B. 203–A. 204–C. 205–D. 206–C. 207–A. 208–A. 209–B. 210–C. 211–None of them: a peacock does not lay eggs. 212–D. 213–B. 214–D.

---

215 Who are, or were, Gambino, Genovese, Colombo, Bonanno and Lucchese?
A. Fictional detectives
B. Victims of poisoning by the Borgias
C. The five Mafia families of New York
D. Characters in Shakespearian comedies

216 What has rapidly become known as, 'the Formula 1 bathchair'?
A. The Robin Reliant B. The Ford Invicta
C. The Hewlett-Packard Mark VI D. Clive Sinclair's C 5

217 What is a billycock'?
A. A type of hat
B. A camper's all-purpose food and drink mug
C. A male goat
D. A type of four-wheeled bicycle

218 The Chinese game Tsu Chu was the first form of which popular game?
A. Bridge B. Tennis C. Rugby D. Soccer

219 How many murders are firmly attributed to Jack the Ripper?
A. 5 B. 10 C. 15 D. 20

220 Of which famous playwright was Mary Arden the mother?
A. William Shakespeare B. George Bernard Shaw
C. Oscar Wilde D. Tennessee Williams

221 Alan Price originally became famous as a member of which group?
A. The Who B. The Monkees
C. The Animals D. The Dave Clark Five

222 Who wrote, 'I must have been an insufferable child; all children are'?
A. Jean-Paul Sartre B. W C Fields
C. Oscar Wilde D. Dorothy Parker

223 How many names were contained in the very first telephone directory to be compiled?
A. 50 B. 100 C. 500 D. 1 000

224 In which county is the village of Upper Wriggle Brook?
A. Hertfordshire B. Dorset
C. Cornwall D. Herefordshire

225 Who was known as the 'Sock-it-to-me' girl, from using the phrase repeatedly on Rowan and Martin's 'Laugh-In'?
A. Goldie Hawn B. Judy Carne
C. Lily Tomlin D. Gracie Allen

226 What was the surname of the gamekeeper in 'Lady Chatterley's Lover'?
A. Connors B. Brown C. Mellors D. Willis

227 Of which American President was Nancy Hanks the mother?
A. Richard Nixon B. George Washington
C. Thomas Jefferson D. Abraham Lincoln

228 In which year was soccer's first World Cup held?
A. 1920 B. 1930 C. 1946 D. 1952

229 What nationality was England's very first Poet Laureate?
A. English B. French C. Irish D. German

ANSWERS pages 40–41: 215–C. 216–D. 217–A. 218–D. 219–A. 220–A. 221–C. 222–C. 223–A. 224–D. 225–B. 226–C. 227–D. 228–B. 229–B

---

230 What is the highest hereditary title of the British peerage?
A. Earl B. Baron C. Duke D. Viscount

231 Who is, or was, William of Arethyn?
A. A legendary Welsh King who defended Offa's Dyke against the English invaders
B. An Old English Sheepdog who dabbled on the Stock Exchange and beat the Inland Revenue
C. The husband of Queen Charlotte of Arcady
D. A pedigree tortoise who won the 'Turtle of the Year' award in 1984

232 Which boxer was nicknamed the 'Wild Bull of the Pampas'?
A. Luis Firpo B. Joe Louis
C. Primo Carnera D. Joe Walcott

233 'We Fly the World the Way the World Wants to Fly' was a slogan of which airline?
A. Pan Am B. TWA
C. Braniff D. Singapore Airlines

234 Which Italian town is the home of violin-making?
A. Cremona B. Milan C. Genoa D. Florence

235 Where would you find the crater Bessel?
A. Peru B. Lanzarote C. Crete D. The Moon

236 Which city is associated with the special green colour worn by Robin Hood?
A. Nottingham B. Lincoln C. Chester D. Hereford

237 Who was the King of England at the time of the Gunpowder Plot?
A. James I B. Henry II C. George III D. Edward IV

238 Which singer often answered his telephone with the name John Burrows when he didn't want to be in when he was?
A. Enrico Caruso B. Elvis Presley
C. Jimi Hendrix D. Tom Jones

239 For what was butter originally used?
A. Cooking B. As an ointment
C. As a lubricant D. As a primitive form of glue

240 Which American inventor said, 'Genius is one per cent inspiration and ninety-nine per cent perspiration'?
A. Benjamin Franklin B. Samuel Morse
C. Thomas Edison D. Alexander Graham Bell

241 Who is the famous daughter of Hilda Acheson?
A. Margot Fonteyn B. Ingrid Bergman
C. Myra Hess D. Margaret Thatcher

242 Who was the first woman on earth, according to Greek mythology?
A. Eve B. Pandora C. Osiris D. Desdemona

243 What happened to the victims of defenestration?
A. They were castrated
B. Their hair was shaved off
C. They were exiled
D. They were thrown through windows

244 For which football club was Alex James a star in the 1930s?
A. Liverpool B. Tottenham Hotspur
C. Arsenal D. Wolverhampton Wanderers

ANSWERS pages 42–43: 230–C. 231–B. 232–A. 233–A. 234–A. 235–D. 236–B. 237–A. 238–B. 239–B. 240–C. 241–A. 242–B. 243–D. 244–C.

---

245 Which Minister of Transport introduced the breathalyser to Britain?
A. Shirley Williams B. Dr Beeching
C. Barbara Castle D. Ernest Marples

246 Who wrote the novel on which Gershwin's 'Porgy and Bess' was based?
A. Mark Twain B. DuBose Heyward
C. Robert Shaw D. Ernest Hemingway

247 To whom was Passepartout valet?
A. Inspector Clouseau B. Sherlock Holmes
C. Bertie Wooster D. Phileas Fogg

248 Approximately how many total hours of music (playing time) did Beethoven compose during his lifetime?
A. 80 B. 120 C. 180 D. 320

249 What took place in Spitsbergen in 1894 – at midnight?
A. A cricket match, organised by the Earl of Sheffield
B. A golf tournament, organised by Lord Tollemache
C. The start of a Monte Carlo rally for coach and four, organised by Lord Wycombe
D. A polo match, organised by Lord Cowdray

250 In Scotland, which is the main centre for the production of cashmere garments?
A. Perth B. Hawick C. Aberdeen D. Edinburgh

251 Is Indaba a Zulu . . .?

A. War dance B. Marriage ceremony
C. Tribal Conference D. War party

252 Who is the famous son of Pauline Koch?
A. Menachem Begin B. Albert Schweitzer
C. Albert Einstein D. David Ben Gurion

253 In which 1967 film was James Bond played by David Niven?
A. Thunderball B. Casino Royale
C. You Only Live Twice D. Diamonds Are Forever

254 Cu is the symbol for which chemical element?
A. Bronze B. Gold C. Copper D. Tungsten

255 Which is the smallest state in the USA?
A. Rhode Island B. Hawaii
C. Utah D. South Carolina

256 How many International Time Zones are there?
A. 1 B. 6 C. 12 D. 24

257 By what more colloquial name is the plant Dicentra Spectabilis known?
A. Ragwort B. Love Lies Bleeding
C. Bleeding Heart D. Deadly Nightshade

258 On which nation did Algeria declare war in 1967, but didn't actually send any troops into battle?
A. Saudi Arabia B. Tibet C. Israel D. Iran

259 Which is the biggest wine-producing country in South America?
A. Argentina B. Venezuela C. Bolivia D. Peru

260 How many of Henry VIII's wives were beheaded?
A. 1 B. 2 C. 3 D. 4

ANSWERS pages 44–45: 245–C. 246–B. 247–D. 248–B. 249–A. 250–B. 251–C. 252–C. 253–B. 254–C. 255–A. 256–D. 257–C. 258–C. 259–A. 260–B.

---

261 Under what title was the book originally called 'Come and Go' published?
A. Portnoy's Complaint B. Catch-22
C. The Happy Hooker D. Sons and Lovers

262 Of which famous film star was Gladys Hogan the mother?
A. Jean Harlow B. Diana Dors
C. Raquel Welch D. Marilyn Monroe

263 Who was the first British king to visit a public theatre?
A. Charles I B. Charles II
C. Henry VII D. Henry VIII

264 Which was the first city in the world to grow to a population of one million?
A. New York B. Tokyo C. London D. Chicago

265 Which is the last book of the Bible?
A. Revelations B. Malachi C. Joshua D. Job

266 Where was the 1984 Labour Party Conference held?
A. Brighton B. Blackpool
C. Birmingham D. Porthcawl

267 On what date was Black Tuesday, the day of the Wall Street Crash?
A. February 2, 1927 B. June 6, 1928
C. October 29, 1929 D. November 11, 1931

268 How many film versions of R L Stevenson's 'Dr Jekyll and Mr Hyde' have been made?
A. Between 5 and 15 B. Between 16 and 30
C. Between 31 and 40 D. Over 40

269 To what age did Methuselah live, according to the Bible?
A. 296 B. 569 C. 969 D. 1 996

270 Perpetually how old is Popeye?
A. 24 B. 34 C. 44 D. 54

271 What is Quadwrangle?
A. A film B. A type of courtyard
C. A game played with dice D. An Eastern sweetmeat

272 When did Concorde first carry fare-paying passengers?
A. 1970 B. 1973 C. 1976 D. 1979

273 Who invented the vacuum cleaner?
A. J Edgar Hoover, in 1929
B. An unknown Russian inventor, in 1926
C. J Murray Spangler, in 1908
D. Mr 'Electrolux' Brown, in 1921

274 Why was Easter Island in the Pacific so named?
A. It was discovered by a sea captain named Easter
B. At the time it was thought to be the furthest point East so far discovered
C. It was discovered on Easter day
D. From the French 'Est-ce que?' – 'Is that an island?'

275 Who was the first tennis player to achieve the Grand Slam twice?
A. Bill Tilden B. Jack Kramer
C. Lew Hoad D. Rod Laver

276 Where, in 1883, was the first skyscraper built?
A. Tokyo B. New York C. Chicago D. Los Angeles

ANSWERS pages 46–47: 261–C. 262–D. 263–B. 264–C. 265–A. 266–B. 267–C. 268–D. 269–C. 270–B. 271–C. 272–C. 273–C. 274–C. 275–D. 276–C

---

277 In 1981, which actor or actress won the Oscar for Best Director – for the first film that he/she ever directed?
A. Robert Redford B. Barbra Streisand
C. Omar Sharif D. Lynne Redgrave

278 Which is America's oldest organised sport?
A. Ice-Hockey B. Baseball
C. American Football D. Lacrosse

279 Which was the first book ever to be prepared on a typewriter?
A. 'The Adventures of Tom Sawyer' by Mark Twain
B. 'A Christmas Carol' by Charles Dickens
C. 'Alice in Wonderland' by Lewis Carroll
D. 'The Great Gatsby' by Scott Fitzgerald

280 Yuri Gagarin, the first ever man in space who returned to tell the tale, was killed in 1968. How did he die?
A. He was killed by a car in the streets of Moscow while on the way to a reception in his honour
B. In an attempt to land on Venus, his spacecraft blew up shortly after take-off
C. He died in an air crash
D. He was killed by muggers

281 Name the massive cannon used by Germany to bombard Paris in World War One.
A. Big Bessie B. Big Greta
C. Big Brunhilde D. Big Bertha

282 In which city was America's Liberty Bell manufactured?
A. New York B. Paris C. London D. Brussels

283 What is Emerson Fittipaldi's sport?
A. Tennis B. Golf C. Cycling D. Motor-racing

284 Where is Napoleon Bonaparte buried?
A. Elba B. St Helena C. Paris D. Corsica

285 Who, created by Charles Schulz, plays Beethoven's works on a toy piano?
A. Charlie Brown B. Linus C. Marcie D. Schroeder

286 Paul Shane plays camp host Ted Bovis in the popular TV series 'Hi-de-Hi'. What was his former profession?
A. Singer B. Miner C. Teacher D. Barman

287 Who succeeds Macbeth as king in Shakespeare's play?
A. Macduff B. Banquo C. Malcolm D. Donalbain

288 In which sport for amateurs is the Walker Cup awarded?
A. Cricket B. Squash C. Table-tennis D. Golf

289 Who met at the Criterion Bar in 1881, for the first time?
A. Sherlock Holmes and Dr Watson
B. Sherlock Holmes and Professor Moriarty
C. Samuel Pepys and Dr Johnson
D. Charles Dickens and R B Sheridan

290 In which country would you pay in quetzals?
A. Nigeria B. Malaya C. Burma D. Guatemala

291 In which American city is the Trivia Hall of Fame situated?
A. Chicago, Illinois B. Austin, Texas
C. Lincoln, Nebraska D. Memphis, Tennessee

ANSWERS pages 48–49: 277–A. 278–D. 279–A. 280–C. 281–D. 282–C. 283–D. 284–C. 285–D. 286–B. 287–C. 288–D. 289–A. 290–D. 291–C.

---

292 Of what is oology the study?
A. Mud B. Eggs C. Eels D. The ozone layer in the atmosphere

293 Which South American country has two capitals?
A. Venezuela B. Brazil C. Bolivia D. Peru

294 What is the title of James Joyce's one and only play?
A. Ulysses B. She Stoops to Conquer
C. Manhattan D. Exiles

295 What did Davy Crockett call his rifle?
A. Old Faithful B. Old Betsy
C. Doris D. The Fireman

296 If you ordered an oyster in a butcher's shop, with what type of meat would you be served?
A. Pork B. Beef C. Veal D. Lamb

297 The Lords Test Match of 1934 became known as 'Verity's Match' because of the number of Australian wickets that Verity took in one day. How many?
A. 8 B. 10 C. 12 D. 14

298 How many bottles of champagne are contained in a Jeroboam?
A. 2 B. 4 C. 8 D. 16

299 Where is the World Toy Fair held annually?
A. New York B. London C. Nuremberg D. Paris

300 Which was the last part of France that the French recaptured from the English in 1558?
A. Paris B. Marseilles C. Lyons D. Calais

301 In which American police series is Mike Stone a cop?
A. Hill Street Blues B. Starsky and Hutch
C. Cagney and Lacy D. The Streets of San Francisco

302 To date, Alfred Packer is the only man in the US to have been convicted of which crime?
A. Cannibalism
B. White slave-trafficking
C. Kidnapping of a tax official
D. Murdering his wife for playing a bridge hand badly

303 By what name is the murderer David Berkowitz known?
A. The Boston Strangler B. Son of Sam
C. The Yorkshire Ripper D. The Boy Butcher

304 In which country are road distances measured in versts?
A. Antarctica B. Tibet C. Ethiopia D. Russia

305 Whom did James Earl Ray shoot and kill in 1969?
A. John F Kennedy B. Robert Kennedy
C. Martin Luther King D. Mary Jo Kopechne

306 Which UN General Secretary was killed in 1961?
A. Trygve Lie B. U Thant
C. Dag Hammarskjold D. Henry Kissinger

307 Michael Quinn was the first Englishman to hold which post?
A. Head Chef at the Ritz
B. Boxing trainer to Joe Frazier
C. Treasurer of the Bank of Dubai
D. Manager of Fortnum and Mason's food department

ANSWERS pages 50–51: 292–B. 293–C. 294–D. 295–B. 296–C. 297–D. 298–B. 299–C. 300–D. 301–D. 302–A. 303–B. 304–D. 305–C. 306–C.(In an aircrash) 307–A.

---

308 Which is the largest state in the USA?
A. Texas B. California C. Florida D. Alaska

309 In Ancient Greece, what was the name given to the place where chariots were raced?
A. Velodrome B. Colosseum
C. Hippodrome D. Basilodrome

310 Which football team won the European Cup in 1984 for the fourth time?
A. Liverpool B. Manchester United
C. Tottenham Hotspur D. Arsenal

311 What was the name of the 1976 film that was based on the novel by Jack Higgins and featured a plot to kidnap Churchill?
A. The Eagle Has Landed B. Who Dares, Wins
C. From Here to Eternity D. The Long Road

312 Normally, how old is a Jewish boy when he celebrates his Barmitzvah?
A. 11 B. 13 C. 15 D. 17

313 Who committed the first ever cycling offence?
A. Kirkpatrick Macmillan, the inventor of the bicycle, who ran over a child who had run into his path to see the curious machine go by
B. The unnamed man who stole the first bicycle from its inventor

C. The very first manufacturer, who did not put brakes on the machines
D. The girlfriend of the inventor, who illegally rode on the crossbar while the inventor was pedalling, sitting in the saddle

314 Who wrote the famous trilogy, 'The Once and Future King'?
A. T H White B. A J P Taylor
C. J R R Tolkien D. P Howard

315 To which note does a symphony orchestra tune?
A. A B. B C. C D. D

316 Who, in 1980, said, 'I am not interested in a third party. I do not believe that it has any future'?
A. David Owen B. Bill Rodgers
C. Margaret Thatcher D. Shirley Williams

317 In 1934, how did film star Clark Gable cause confusion in the underwear manufacturing market?
A. Because, in his latest film, he obviously wore no vest under his shirt, and this fashion was slavishly copied by thousands of film-goers, to the detriment of the vest manufacturers
B. Because, on screen, his vest was seen to be torn to shreds comparatively easily; others did the same, and thousands were returned to the vest manufacturers, with demands for refund
C. Because he wore jockey type underpants, which thousands of film-goers now wanted to purchase. Unfortunately, most manufacturers only made the trunk style, which they now could not sell
D. Because he wore a string vest. These were not on general sale at the time, and the manufacturers could not cope with the demand, having already stockpiled 'regular' vests ready for the forthcoming winter

ANSWERS pages 52–53: 308–D. 309–C. 310–A. 311–A. 312–B. 313–A. 314–A. 315–A. 316–D. 317–A.

---

318 Which instrument normally plays the note to which a symphony orchestra tunes?
A. Violin B. Oboe C. Clarinet D. Trumpet

319 What is Latin for 'left'?
A. Leftus B. Linkus C. Sinister D. Lupus

320 Who recorded the fastest tennis serve, clocked at 154 mph?
A. Roscoe Tanner B. John McEnroe
C. Bob Falkenberg D. Mike Sangster

321 Which famous French artist painted scenes of Parisian life from the Moulin Rouge nightclub?
A. Gauguin B. Manet
C. Audubon D. Toulouse-Lautrec

322 Who composed the music to 'West Side Story' and was also resident conductor of the New York Philharmonic from 1958–1969?
A. André Previn B. Arthur Fiedler
C. Leonard Bernstein D. John Williams

323 Who were the Huguenots?
A. French Catholic supporters of Napoleon
B. French Agnostic supporters of Napoleon
C. French Protestant supporters of Calvin
D. French Agnostic supporters of Calvin

324 Of which country is Keflavik the largest airport?
A. Poland B. Yugoslavia
C. Czechoslovakia D. Iceland

325 What speed at sea level is MACH 1?
A. 550 mph B. 760 mph
C. 1 000 mph D. 1 570 mph

326 Who were the mythological founders of Rome?
A. Castor and Pollux B. Romulus and Remus
C. Gog and Magog D. Hengis and Horsa

327 Which US President did Leon Czolgosz kill?
A. Abraham Lincoln B. William McKinley
C. Andrew Jackson D. John F Kennedy

328 What are the two colours of the flag of the United Nations?
A. Blue and white B. Red and white
C. Red and blue D. Blue and yellow

329 Who was the 'Come Outside girl' from Mike Sarne's No 1 hit?
A. Wendy Richard B. Joan Collins
C. Lulu D. Dusty Springfield

330 Where do Norwich City FC play their home matches?
A. Motspur Park B. The Dell
C. Elland Road D. Carrow Road

331 Whose last words were, 'Oh, I am so bored with it all'?
A. Napoleon B. Queen Victoria
C. Sir Winston Churchill D. Picasso

332 Where does London Bridge now stand?
A. Skokie, Illinois, USA
B. Bethesda, Maryland, USA
C. Tokyo, Japan
D. Lake Havasu City, Arizona, USA

ANSWERS pages 54–55: 318–B. 319–C. 320–D. 321–D. 322–C. 323–C. 324–D. 325–B. 326–B. 327–B. 328–A. 329–A. 330–D. 331–C. 332–D.

---

333 What was the American General Stilwell's nickname?
A. Vinegar Joe B. Old Ironsides
C. Blood and Guts D. Stonewall

334 What was Ethiopia previously called?
A. Abyssinia B. Persia C. Bechuanaland D. Gaul

335 Who is the High Chief of Manus, a South Pacific island?
A. The Poet Laureate (by tradition) B. Adam Faith
C. Sir Stanley Matthews D. Prince Charles

336 How many pints can the average human stomach hold?
A. 2 B. 4 C. 6 D. 8

337 Which American city is nicknamed 'City of Brotherly Love'?
A. Salt Lake City B. Boston
C. Philadelphia D. Indianapolis

338 Which chemical element is represented by the formula Na?
A. Sodium B. Nitrogen C. Nickel D. Zinc

339 What symbol or symbols is depicted on the Canadian flag?
A. A maple leaf
B. A maple leaf and star
C. A maple leaf in a circle
D. A maple leaf, six stars and six stripes

340 Jimi Hendrix and Janis Joplin both died at what age?
A. 22 B. 25 C. 27 D. 31

341 What did American Dan Fletcher invent?
A. A motorised baby buggy
B. A carhorn that gives out messages in morse code
C. A computer that reads a book out loud
D. A motorised pogo-stick

342 What is the capital of Argentina?
A. Buenos Aires B. Sao Paulo
C. Caracas D. Guatemala

343 Which Nazi was calling himself Klement Ricardo and living in Argentina when he was captured in 1960 by the Israelis?
A. Martin Bormann B. Dr Mengele C. Albert Speers D. Adolph Eichmann

344 At what age did Horatio Nelson first go to sea?
A. 9 B. 12 C. 15 D. 18

345 Who composed the Haydn, or St Anthony Variations?
A. Beethoven B. Brahms
C. Mozart D. Mendelssohn

346 The Government agreed in 1985 to raise deposits at Parliamentary elections to £500 from what?
A. £100 B. £150 C. £200 D. £250

347 What was the name of the riderless horse that marched in the funeral procession of President John F Kennedy?
A. Diamond B. Black Jack C. Poker D. Sapphire

348 In which year was the last mule de-mobbed by the British Army?
A. 1945 B. 1955 C. 1965 D. 1975

349 Who played Don Corleone in 'The Godfather'?
A. Ernest Borgnine B. Burt Lancaster
C. James Mason D. Marlon Brando

ANSWERS pages 56–57: 333–A. 334–A. 335–D. 336–B. 337–C. 338–A. 339–A. 340–C. 341–D. 342–A. 343–D. 344–B. 345–B. 346–B. 347–B. 348–D. 349–D.

---

350 Of what are Ogen, Canteloupe and Honeydew all types?
A. Lemons B. Yams C. Tomatoes D. Melons

351 How many martyrs were deported for striking from the Dorset village of Tolpuddle, in 1831?
A. 6 B. 12 C. 18 D. 24

352 If a stamp contains the word Suomi, from which country does it originate?
A. Sweden B. Swaziland C. Finland D. Switzerland

353 Nicholas Breakspear has been the only English Pope to date, and he died from drinking a cup of wine. Why?
A. Because it was just one cup too many
B. Because there was a fly in the glass, and he choked to death on it
C. Because the wine was poisoned
D. Because he had developed an allergy to wine

354 Why were bowler hats so called?
A. Because they were originally invented as a protection for batsmen from fast bowlers, but cricketers rejected the idea
B. They were originally made by the hatmaking company of Thomas and William Bowler
C. Because they were made round and bowl-shaped
D. Because of the way that they bowled away when the wind blew them off

355 Of which precious metal was the Mildenhall Treasure made?
A. Gold B. Silver C. Platinum D. Cupro-nickel

356 Which disease do mosquitoes carry?
A. Cholera B. Typhoid C. Beri-Beri D. Malaria

357 In which two cities is Charles Dickens's novel 'A Tale of Two Cities' set?
A. London and Paris B. London and Rome
C. Paris and Rome D. Paris and Lyons

358 The Beatles gave their final concert on August 29, 1966. Where was it held?
A. The Cavern, Liverpool
B. Central Park, New York
C. Candlestick Park, San Francisco
D. The Hollywood Bowl

359 Who is Hamlet's mother?
A. Ophelia B. Maud C. Gertrude D. Cecilia

360 When did traffic wardens first appear in England?
A. 1955 B. 1960 C. 1965 D. 1970

361 Apart from man, which is the only other breed of animal to get sunburnt?
A. Dogs B. Pigs C. Horses D. Cows

362 In which of Sir Arthur Conan Doyle's stories did Sherlock Holmes first say the words, 'Elementary, my dear Watson'?
A. Sign of Four
B. The Speckled Band
C. The Sussex Vampire
D. He never actually used this line

363 Who were the first to use fingerprints for identification?
A. Russians B. Chinese C. Americans D. British

364 Of what is arachnophobia the fear?
A. Dark B. Water C. Rats D. Spiders

ANSWERS pages 58–59: 350–D. 351–A. 352–C. 353–B. 354–B. 355–B. 356–D. 357–A. 358–C. 359–C. 360–B. 361–B. 362–D. 363–B. 364–D

---

365 What was the Gordon Bennett Trophy Race?
A. The first ever international motor race run in Britain, in 1903
B. The annual booby-prize stock car race for drivers who have never previously won an event
C. A distance or duration race for battery operated boats
D. The advertising slogan balloon race, each company being allowed 10 balloons, specially numbered, and the accompanying card returned from the longest distance by the time of the following year's meeting, gets the prize

366 In which film did Jack Torrence repeatedly type the line, 'All work and no play makes Jack a dull boy'?
A. The Shining B. The Graduate
C. The Exorcist D. The Manchurian Candidate

367 What is the most common street name in the USA?
A. Madison B. Park C. Lincoln D. Washington

368 Alice Wells joined which Los Angeles force in 1910 to become the world's first female what?
A. Fireman B. Public Prosecutor
C. Female Ambulance driver D. Police officer

369 In which year was Britain's first premium bond draw held?
A. 1955 B. 1957 C. 1959 D. 1961

370 Which of these cities has *not* hosted the Summer Olympic Games?

A. Munich B. New York C. London D. Rome

371 US Army General McAuliffe made a very succinct reply to the German request to surrender at the Battle of the Bulge in 1944. What was it?
A. 'Nuts' B. !!! (ie unprintable)
C. 'Go to Hell' D. 'Bullshit'

372 'That was the best ice cream soda I ever tasted.' These were the last words ever spoken by which comedian, who died in 1959?
A. Jack Benny B. Lenny Bruce
C. Lou Costello D. Stan Laurel

373 Port of Spain is the capital of which Caribbean island?
A. Jamaica B. Trinidad C. St Lucia D. St Kitts

374 Which trio were named Curly, Larry and Moe?
A. The Three Degrees B. The Three Musketeers
C. The Trio Los Paramos D. The Three Stooges

375 What is the top rifle shooting contest at Bisley?
A. The Queen's Prize
B. The Duke of Edinburgh Award
C. Cracksman of the Year
D. Army, Navy and Air-Force Premier Prize

376 Which is the largest ocean in the world?
A. Atlantic B. Indian C. Arctic D. Pacific

377 From where does the dish 'chop suey' originate?
A. Peking B. Canton C. New York D. Manchester

378 How many people used London's first ever public lavatory during the first month in which it was opened, in 1852?
A. 82 B. 473 C. 826 D. 1 596

ANSWERS pages 60–61: 365–A. 366–A. 367–B. 368–D. 369–B. 370–B. 371–A. 372–C. 373–B. 374–D. 375–A. 376–D. 377–C. 378–A.

---

379 Which is the earliest known printed book, dating from May 11, 868?
A. Diamond Sutra B. Gutenberg Bible
C. King James Bible D. Kama Sutra

380 With what is cointreau flavoured?
A. Apples B. Pears C. Oranges D. Lemons

381 A Yarborough is a hand of cards containing no card above what?
A. 8 B. 9 C. 10 D. Jack

382 Who coined the word 'scrooge'?
A. John Donne B. Geoffrey Chaucer
C. Charles Dickens D. John Bunyan

383 What is the highest score obtainable for a hand of five cards at cribbage?
A. 24 B. 29 C. 32 D. 36

384 How many cards are in a set of Continuo?
A. 24 B. 36 C. 42 D. 52

385 At what game was Alekhine a world champion?
A. Draughts B. Bridge C. Go D. Chess

386 In which year was the tax on windows, introduced in 1696, abolished?
A. 1701 B. 1751 C. 1801 D. 1851

387 How many pieces does each player have at Backgammon at the beginning of a game? (As normally played in the UK.)
A. 15 B. 20 C. 25 D. 30

388 What was the result of the 1984 cricket Test series England v the West Indies?
A. England was 3–2 B. A draw
C. West Indies won 3–2 D. West Indies won 5–0

389 As what was coffee originally drunk?
A. For the same purposes as today
B. To ward off evil spirits during the 16th century
C. As a medicine
D. As a welcome drink for travellers

390 In which year did man first fly faster than the speed of sound?
A. 1941 B. 1951 C. 1961 D. 1971

391 Who is generally credited with having composed the song 'Greensleeves'?
A. Purcell B. King Henry VIII C. King David
D. Mozart

392 What was the famous sign on the desk of USA President Harry S Truman?
A. What I say, goes
B. The buck stops here
C. Think, think, then think again
D. You can take that as a definite maybe

393 Al Jolson died after a heart attack in 1950. It occurred while he was playing which game?
A. Poker B. Golf C. Tennis D. Bridge

394 What normally signifies sharpness of vision in Britain?
A. 1/1 B. 6/6 C. 20/20 D. 100/100

ANSWERS pages 62–63: 379–A. 380–C. 381–B. 382–C. 383–B. 384–C. 385–D. 386–D. 387–A. 388–D. 389–C. 390–A. 391–B. 392–B. 393–A. 394–B

---

395 The leader of which religious group is often referred to as the Black Pope?
A. Mormons B. Jesuits
C. Plymouth Brethren D. Salvation Army

396 What normally signifies sharpness of vision in the USA?
A. 1/1 B. 6/6 C. 20/20 D. 100/100

397 Where was Sir Winston Churchill's mother born?
A. England B. Scotland C. France D. USA

398 According to the Bible, what is the root of all evil?
A. Money B. The love of money
C. Woman D. Serpents

399 Who was the first man to hit a golf ball on the moon?
A. Neil Armstrong B. Michael Collins
C. Alan Shepard D. Buzz Aldrin

400 Which treaty ended the American Revolution?
A. The Treaty of Paris B. The Treaty of Rome
C. The Treaty of Versailles D. The Treaty of Toronto

401 Who, in mythology, ferried folk across the River Styx?
A. Bunyan B. Charon C. Beelzebub D. Lucifer

402 What colour are the bells on a one-armed bandit?
A. Red B. Blue C. Green D. Yellow

403 In which year was Sputnik 1, the first satellite in space, launched?

A. 1955 B. 1957 C. 1959 D. 1961

404 'Blood and Fire' is the motto of which army?
A. The US Army B. The PLO
C. The Israeli Army D. The Salvation Army

405 Which new article of clothing does Michael Jackson wear for each show in which he performs?
A. A specially made tie
B. A glove on his right hand
C. A hand-monogrammed shirt
D. A black handkerchief

406 Who succeeded Vic Feather as General Secretary of the TUC?
A. Aneurin Bevan B. Len Murray
C. Bill Sirs D. Arthur Scargill

407 Doctors Bob and Bill founded which organisation in 1935?
A. Gamblers Anonymous B. Alcoholics Anonymous
C. Diners Club D. The Samaritans

408 Who immediately preceded Sir Alec Douglas Home as Britain's Prime Minister?
A. Harold Wilson B. Edward Heath
C. Clement Attlee D. Harold Macmillan

409 Champagne and stout are the ingredients of which drink?
A. Manhattan B. Sidecar
C. Black Velvet D. Bloody Mary

410 By what name is Jean Chauvin, who was born in 1509, now remembered?
A. Thomas Cromwell B. John Calvin
C. Louis XIV D. James I

ANSWERS pages 64–65: 395–B. 396–C. 397–D. 398–B. 399–C. 400–A. 401–B. 402–D. 403–B. 404–D. 405–B. 406–B. 407–B. 408–D. 409–C. 410–B.

---

411 Newton Heath became which famous soccer team?
A. Manchester United B. Manchester City
C. Liverpool D. Everton

412 Of which gas is Mars's atmosphere thought to be chiefly composed?
A. Hydrogen B. Carbon Dioxide
C. Oxygen D. Sulphur Dioxide

413 Which monster did Beowulf kill?
A. Grendel B. Cyclops C. Hydra D. Perseus

414 Richard Strauss used an unusual instrument in his work 'Don Quixote' and suggested that it might be better if it were played off-stage to prevent the audience laughing. What was it?
A. An alpenhorn – the very long variety
B. A wind machine
C. A collection of crockery to be smashed at appropriate points in the score
D. A type of xylophone made from wine bottles

415 Which Hungarian composer took holy orders in 1865?
A. Liszt B. Brahms C. Bartok D. Kodaly

416 How many wickets did Harold Larwood take for England in the infamous 'Bodyline' series of 1932–33?
A. 23 B. 28 C. 33 D. 38

417 Name Roy Rogers's famous horse.

A. Champion B. Trigger C. Lassie D. Pinto

418 At age 13, Michael Adams of Cornwall is the youngest in the world ever to achieve what distinction?
A. The rank of Lifemaster on the English Bridge Union register
B. A high jump of 6′6″
C. Swimming the English Channel in both directions
D. A rating of 2 400 on the International Chess Federation Scale

419 Of whom is St Hubert the patron saint?
A. Cobblers B. Money lenders
C. Hunters D. Musicians

420 Which is the city of 'dreaming spires'?
A. Bath B. Canterbury C. Oxford D. Cambridge

421 What was the occupation of 1980 BBC 'Mastermind' Fred Housego?
A. Traindriver B. Schoolteacher
C. Solicitor D. Taxi driver

422 In a standard pack of playing cards, what does the King of Spades carry in his left hand?
A. Nothing B. A glass C. A sword D. A quill pen

423 Of what is calligraphy the art?
A. Handwriting B. Engraving
C. Painting D. Book-binding

424 Who led the Romans to Britain in 55BC?
A. Nero B. Claudius C. Tiberius D. Julius Caesar

425 Who wrote the music for 'Stardust'?
A. Irving Berlin B. Cole Porter
C. Hoagy Carmichael D. George Gershwin

ANSWERS pages 66–67: 411–A. 412–B. 413–A. 414–B. 415–A. 416–C. 417–B. 418–D. 419–C. 420–C. 421–D. 422–C. 423–A. 424–D. 425–C

---

426 For which group of people did Levi Strauss make the first jeans, in 1850?
A. For gold diggers in the Californian gold rush
B. For American railway workers
C. For cowboys
D. As hardwearing trousers for ranch-hands

427 What kind of flower is an Ena Harkness?
A. Rose B. Tulip C. Hyacinth D. Lupin

428 From which country does the harmonica, or mouth-organ, originate?
A. France B. America C. India D. Germany

429 What other first did Neil Armstrong, the first man on the moon, achieve?
A. He was the first astronaut to be elected as a US senator
B. He won the first marathon race for astronauts
C. He was on board during the first docking in space between a manned and an unmanned spacecraft
D. He was the first astronaut to be made a judge

430 Who is the Merchant of Venice?
A. Shylock B. Antonio C. Portia D. Jessica

431 Which world heavyweight boxing champion's opponents weighed more than him in every one of his title contests?
A. Muhammad Ali B. Joe Louis
C. Sonny Liston D. Rocky Marciano

432 From which country does Emerson Fittipaldi come?
A. Brazil B. Italy C. USA D. Australia

433 Who is the Scarlet Pimpernel?
A. Sam Spade B. Percy Blakeney
C. Michael Milsom D. James Hilton

434 What is a cross between a zebra and a donkey called?
A. A zebry B. A donzey C. A zonkey D. A zeekee

435 When did the first launderette open – it was in America?
A. 1928 B. 1934 C. 1942 D. 1956

436 Who is Makepeace's American partner?
A. Sullivan B. Brown C. McDonald D. Dempsey

437 Rorschach of Switzerland gave his name to a psychiatric test concerned with what?
A. Rats B. Dreams C. Ink blots D. Wooden shapes

438 What is the Haus der Kunst, in Munich?
A. A house of ill-repute
B. The main courthouse
C. An art gallery
D. A specially constructed indoor swimming pool for use by the disabled

439 What is the capital of Queensland, Australia?
A. Canberra B. Adelaide C. Sydney D. Brisbane

440 Which country has its own map on its flag?
A. Turkey B. Cyprus C. Greece D. Sardinia

441 What piece of music did Ravel compose for the dancer Ida Rubinstein?
A. Rustle of Spring B. Bolero
C. La Mer D. The Polovtsian Dances

ANSWERS pages 68–69: 426–A. 427–A. 428–D. 429–C. 430–B. 431–D. 432–A. 433–B. 434–C. 435–B. 436–D. 437–C. 438–C. 439–D. 440–B. 441–B.

---

442 What is the name of the largest department store in the Soviet Union?
A. VIM B. CIT C. TASS D. GUM

443 What is the capital of Haiti?
A. Kingston B. Port of Spain
C. Goa D. Port au Prince

444 In which event did Tessa Sanderson achieve a gold medal at the 1984 Olympics?
A. Discus B. Shot C. 200 metres D. Javelin

445 What was US President Cleveland's first name?
A. Frank B. James C. Zachary D. Grover

446 Where in the body is the Eustachian tube?
A. The nose B. The throat
C. The stomach D. The ear

447 What was the name of the very first Jumbo jet to arrive at Heathrow Airport in January 1970?
A. Jumbo 1 B. Clipper Young America
C. King of the Skies D. Atlantic Lounger

448 Name Del-Boy's brother in 'Only Fools and Horses'.
A. Jimmy B. Henry C. Rodney D. Tony

449 Glenn Miller was the first artiste actually to receive a gold record for selling a million copies of one title. What was the record?

A. In the Mood B. Lullaby of Birdland
C. Chattanooga Choo Choo D. Young Man with a Horn

450 On which astrological sign is an archer represented?
A. Sagittarius B. Capricorn C. Aquarius D. Cancer

451 During World War Two, who commanded the German air-force, the Luftwaffe?
A. Goebbels B. Himmler C. Goering D. Eichmann

452 Which is the boxing weight immediately below light-middleweight?
A. Middleweight B. Welterweight
C. Lightweight D. Bantamweight

453 How many points does potting a red score at billiards?
A. 1 B. 2 C. 3 D. 4

454 Which was the first country to have a national flag, in 1219?
A. England B. Italy C. Russia D. Denmark

455 What did Thomas Adams invent, more or less by accident?
A. Elastic bands B. Gob-stoppers
C. Glass eyes D. Chewing gum

456 Who was the first film star ever to appear on a postage stamp?
A. Ronald Reagan B. Grace Kelly
C. Charlie Chaplin D. Rudolph Valentino

457 Whom did Steve Davis beat in the final to win the 1984 Embassy World Snooker Championship?
A. Alex Higgins B. Ray Reardon
C. Jimmy White D. Eddie Charlton

458 Which sport holds competitions in a velodrome?
A. Baseball B. Cycling C. Karate D. Handball

ANSWERS pages 70–71: 442–D. 443–D. 444–D. 445–D. 446–D. 447–B. 448–C. 449–C. 450–A. 451–C. 452–B. 453–C. 454–D. 455–D. 456–B. 457–C. 458–B.

---

459 At what job did Mao Tse-tung originally work?
A. Farm labourer B. Library assistant
C. Schoolteacher D. Water-carrier

460 At which game were Terence Reese and Boris Schapiro World Champions?
A. Chess B. Bridge C. Go D. Draughts

461 Through which two oceans does the International Date Line run?
A. Indian and Pacific B. Atlantic and Arctic
C. Indian and Atlantic D. Pacific and Arctic

462 Who composed the song 'How Deep Is the Ocean'?
A. Ivor Novello B. Irving Berlin
C. Richard Rodgers D. George Gershwin

463 On average, how often does the famous geyser 'Old Faithful' erupt?
A. Once every 13½ minutes
B. Once every 41 minutes
C. Once every 64½ minutes
D. Once every 102 minutes

464 In which city is the Prado Art Gallery?
A. Lisbon B. Prague C. Madrid D. The Hague

465 In World War Two, from what was 'Woolton Pie' made, a dish recommended by the government to help the war effort?

A. Whalemeat B. Corned beef
C. Vegetables D. Dried egg

466 Which American president first used the phrase 'domino theory' in a speech about how Communism might spread through South-East Asia?
A. Eisenhower B. Kennedy C. Johnson D. Nixon

467 About the smells from which industries or firms do the British complain most often to officials?
A. Pig farms B. Maggot farms
C. Knackers' yards D. Tanneries

468 How many years after the murder of Thomas à Becket in Canterbury Cathedral in 1170 was he made a Saint?
A. 3 B. 30 C. 300 D. 504

469 What was the middle name of the actor, singer and playwright Noel Coward?
A. Hobbs B. Pierce C. Miller D. Walton

470 Which saint is said to be particularly good at curing diseases of the eye?
A. St Daniel the Stylite B. St Pancras
C. St Sebastian D. St Lucy

471 What was the claim to fame of Enrico Rastelli, who died in 1937?
A. He was the first juggler to keep ten balls moving in the air at once
B. He was Picasso's favourite male model
C. He was the last man to be publicly guillotined
D. He was the first man to win two Olympic gold medals for boxing

472 What can be caught by 'babbing'?
A. AIDS B. Rats C. Herpes D. Eels

ANSWERS pages 72–73: 459–B. 460–B. 461–D. 462–B. 463–C. 464–C. 465–C. 466–A. 467–B. 468–A. 469–B. 470–D. 471–A. 472–D

---

473 Which novel by Dickens contains a teacher called Mr M'Choakumchild?
A. Hard Times B. Oliver Twist
C. Little Dorrit D. Bleak House

474 What's the second largest castle in Britain, Windsor being the largest?
A. Caernarvon B. Caerphilly
C. Kenilworth D. Edinburgh

475 When the Gunfight at the O K Corral took place in 1881 in Tombstone, Arizona, the law was represented by a marshal and his three deputies. Who was the Marshal?
A. Wyatt Earp B. Morgan Earp
C. Virgil Earp D. Doc Holliday

476 In Chaucer's 'Canterbury Tales', how many husbands did the Wife of Bath have?
A. 3 B. 4 C. 5 D. 6

477 What was the original occupation of the former Poet Laureate, Robert Bridges?
A. Doctor B. Soldier C. Bus-driver D. Jockey

478. When the Australian local newspaper 'The Etheridge Chronicle' had a paper shortage in 1875, what did the editor do?
A. He printed posters to be stuck on to local sheep and kangaroos
B. He employed fifteen loud-mouthed men to read continuously in the street

C. He printed the paper on handkerchiefs instead
D. He printed in extremely small type and gave away magnifying glasses

479 The board game called 'Othello' by the Japanese is a repackaged version of a Victorian game, called what?
A. Black & White B. Capture C. Halma D. Reversi

480 Which novelist's husband became deranged whilst they were on their honeymoon in Venice and jumped from the balcony of their hotel room into the Grand Canal, from which gondoliers rescued him?
A. George Eliot B. Elizabeth Gaskell
C. Virginia Woolf D. Charlotte Brontë

481 In which outdoor game do players use the terms pioneer, pivot and pilot?
A. Lacrosse B. Polo C. Croquet D. Bowls

482 In the slang of a century ago, what was a 'crocus-pitcher'?
A. Street-walking prostitute
B. Quack doctor
C. Member of a pickpocketing gang
D. Unregistered hansom cab

483 Which of these was *not* originally considered a possible title for the television comedy series, 'Monty Python's Flying Circus'?
A. Gwen Dibley's Flying Circus B. A Horse, a Spoon and a Bucket C. Owl Stretching Time D. Brian's Cocoa Factory

484 In what sort of activity do people compete for the Huxley Cup?
A. Flower-arranging B. Hang-gliding
C. Male beauty competition D. Hairdressing

ANSWERS pages 74–75: 473–A. 474–B. 475–C. 476–C. 477–A. 478–C. 479–D. 480–A. 481–C. 482–B. 483–D. 484–A.

---

485 Whom did the poet W B Yeats describe as having 'an ego like a raging tooth'?
A. Bernard Shaw B. Mrs Patrick Campbell
C. Oscar Wilde D. Maud Gonne

486 If you heard an Italian artist was praised for his 'morbidezza', what would you expect to find him doing well? (In his paintings, of course!)
A. Flesh colours B. Dead bodies
C. Women's eyes D. Religious subjects

487 What did Giovanni Schiaparelli believe wrongly that he had discovered in 1877?
A. A cure for rabies B. Canals on Mars
C. Perpetual motion D. Christ's tomb

488 In the Bible, who or what are Pison, Gihon and Hiddekel?
A. Three enemies of Samson B. Three lovers of Jezebel C. Three rivers of Eden D. Three wild beasts of Gilead

489 Which Labour leader said about the James Bond novels that he found the combination of sex, violence and alcohol 'irresistible'?
A. Hugh Gaitskell B. Harold Wilson
C. Michael Foot D. James Callaghan

490 In which book is Muff Potter accused of murdering Doctor Robinson, but saved by the young hero's evidence?
A. Coral Island B. Tom Sawyer

C. The Catcher in the Rye D. To Kill a Mockingbird

491 On what is 'Erskine May' the authority?
A. Early steam engines B. Laws of gambling
C. Parliamentary procedure D. Military drill

492 How many syllables are there in a Japanese poem called a 'haiku'?
A. 12 B. 17 C. 33 D. Between 50 and 60

493 What does a 'fugleman' do?
A. He's a soldier who shows other soldiers how to drill
B. He's a fireman who takes charge at the scene of a major blaze
C. He's a mounted hunter who leads other hunters on foot
D. He's an advance publicity man for a travelling circus

494 In Wales in the 1840s, what did the Rebecca Riots destroy?
A. Weaving machinery B. Railway coal wagons
C. Toll-gates D. Property of slum-owning landlords

495 In Nathaniel Hawthorne's novel, 'The Scarlet Letter', which is the scarlet letter worn by Hester Prynne?
A. A B. B C. C D. D

496 Which country was ruled by Bernardo O'Higgins from 1810 to 1823?
A. Chile B. Ghana C. Goa D. Paraguay

497 Where would you find Aubrey Holes and X and Y holes?
A. Stonehenge B. Avebury
C. Sutton Hoo D. Mildenhall

498 What is a Sabra?
A. A French-built aircraft
B. An Israeli born in Israel
C. A large American plum
D. A female Turkish slave

ANSWERS pages 76–77: 485–B. 486–A. 487–B. 488–C. 489–A. 490–B. 491–C. 492–B. 493–A. 494–C. 495–A.(A for Adultery) 496–A. 497–A. 498–B.

---

499 In which Italian city is the newspaper 'La Stampa' published?
A. Rome B. Naples C. Turin D. Milan

500 Who or what are Judge Roy Scream and the Colossus?
A. Professional wrestlers
B. Alternative comedians
C. American roller-coaster rides
D. Actors in blue movies

501 Who or what are Jumada and Rajab?
A. Two of Mohammed's prophets
B. Cities in Saudi Arabia
C. Names of desert winds
D. Months of the Muslim calendar

502 Which of these independent states is a member of the United Nations?
A. Vietnam B. North Korea
C. South Korea D. Switzerland

503 What were the first names of Mr J Q Hollom, who as Chief Cashier of the Bank of England signed bank notes from 1962 to 1966?
A. John Quentin B. Jasper Quintus
C. Jeremy Quilter D. James Quarmby

504 Who said in 1930, 'It is a good thing for an uneducated man to read books of quotations'?
A. Winston Churchill B. The Prince of Wales

C. Bernard Shaw D. Bertrand Russell

505 Which public office did William Wordsworth hold from 1813 to 1842?
A. Poet Laureate
B. Lord Lieutenant of Cumberland
C. Distributor of Stamps for Westmoreland
D. Official Orator of Oxford University

506 Which unit of the Roman army was one-tenth of a legion?
A. A Maniple B. A century C. An alae D. A cohort

507 What sort of society would a Pantisocracy be?
A. An entirely female group
B. One without organised religion
C. It has complete equality, without rulers
D. One without marriages

508 In George Orwell's '1984', in which of the four Ministries does Winston Smith work?
A. The Ministry of Peace, or Minipax
B. The Ministry of Love, or Miniluv
C. The Ministry of Truth, or Minitrue
D. The Ministry of Plenty, or Miniplenty

509 From what sort of source might a scientist detect Rayleigh waves?
A. Bats B. The Moon
C. A colour television set D. Earthquakes

510 Which of these countries is *not* a member of OPEC, the Organisation of Petroleum Exporting Countries?
A. Venezuela B. Kenya C. Indonesia D. Algeria

511 Which of the Brontë sisters wrote the novel, 'The Tenant of Wildfell Hall'?
A. Emily B. Charlotte C. Elizabeth D. Anne

ANSWERS pages 78–79: 499–D. 500–C. 501–D. 502–A. 503–B. 504–A. 505–C. 506–D. 507–C. 508–C. 509–D. 510–B. 511–D.

---

512 To which famous actor was the actress Rosalind Iden married?
A. Sir Donald Wolfit B. Charles Laughton
C. Robert Donat D. Robert Newton

513 Who was the first Royal baby to be born in Scotland this century, and the first for three hundred years?
A. King George VI B. Queen Elizabeth II
C. Princess Margaret D. The Duke of Windsor

514 Which Old Etonian Prime Minister's maiden speech in Parliament was in defence of the treatment of slaves on his father's plantation in Demerera?
A. The Duke of Wellington B. Gladstone
C. Disraeli D. William Pitt the Younger

515 Why were hand-grenades first called 'grenades'?
A. They were thrown by grenadiers
B. They looked like pomegranates
C. They were invented in Granada
D. The first such bombs were painted green

516 In John Osborne's play, 'Look Back In Anger', how does the hero Jimmy Porter earn his living?
A. He runs a sweet stall in a market
B. He lectures at a university
C. He delivers Sunday papers
D. He lives off the money of his wife, Alison

517 Which city is the meeting-place of the Roman roads Ermine Street and the Fosse Way?

A. Bath B. Chester C. Lincoln D. York

518 With what is the science of orthoepy concerned?
A. The curing of imaginary diseases
B. The measurement of straight lines on curved surfaces
C. Measuring pressures on people to conform to what other people expect
D. The correct pronunciation of words

519 Which King of France died after an accident while jousting in a tournament?
A. Louis II B. Charles II C. Francis II D. Henry II

520 What is the main claim to fame of the 16th-century Jean Nicot, who was French Ambassador to Lisbon?
A. The drug nicotine was named after him
B. He was executed for trying to kill the King of Spain
C. He was the spy who reported the Spanish Armada to England
D. He was the first man to turn potatoes into fried chips

521 What do Americans refer to by the initials 'R V'?
A. A motorised caravan, or recreational vehicle'
B. An ex-soldier, or 'returned veteran'
C. Selling houses, or 'realtor vending'
D. A bounce-shot in basket-ball, or 'returned volley'

522 What do you call the small projection under a hinged seat in a church on which a choir member can rest when standing?
A. Sastrugi B. Pilae C. Misericord D. Corbel

523 Who designed the Argentine flag in 1812?
A. General Malvina B. General Belgrano
C. Comodoro Rivadavia D. General Bahia Blanca

ANSWERS pages 80–81: 512–A. 513–C. 514–B. 515–B. 516–A. 517–C. 518–D. 519–D. 520–A. 521–A. 522–C. 523–B.

---

524 With what would you associate the comma of Didymus and the Pythagorean comma?
A. Butterflies B. Geometry
C. Mixing oil paints D. Tuning musical instruments

525 In manufacturing, what has been removed from steel that is called 'killed' steel?
A. Oxygen B. Impurities C. Silicon D. Mercury

526 Who wrote a poem about the death of his friend Edward King in a shipwreck?
A. Milton B. Byron C. Tennyson D. Shelley

527 When a Rugby League Cup game ends as a draw, how does a referee indicate that extra time is to be played?
A. He points to the centre spot
B. He raises both arms vertically above his head
C. He blows four short blasts on his whistle
D. He extends one arm and swings it from left to right

528 What is meant in economics by 'M-nought'?
A. Bankruptcy B. Debts and assets balance
C. Notes and coins in circulation D. Invisible imports

529 Which country suffered a civil war in the 1840s between Catholics and Protestants that was called the Sonderbund War?
A. Switzerland B. Austria
C. Hungary D. South Africa

530 In geology, what sort of rock makes a batholith?
A. Igneous B. Metamorphic
C. Sedimentary D. Porous

531 In what make of car did John Surtees win the World Motor Racing Drivers' Championship in 1964?
A. Lotus B. Brabham C. Cooper D. Ferrari

532 After the capture of which criminal did American newspapers first call Government agents 'G-men'?
A. 'Ma' Baker B. 'Machine-Gun' Kelly
C. 'Bugs' Moran D. 'Legs' Diamond

533 For what is brachygraphy another term?
A. Shorthand writing B. Tattooing
C. Sports reporting D. Code-breaking

534 In which Caribbean island group did Columbus make his first landfall in the New World?
A. Cayman Islands B. Leeward Islands
C. Windward Islands D. Bahamas

535 What does the British government department called Bona Vacantia do?
A. Deals with unclaimed property after deaths
B. Arranges travel for members of the armed forces
C. Gives permits for exploring archaeological sites
D. Investigates over-manning in the Civil Service

536 What's the name of Britain's tallest lighthouse?
A. Eddystone B. Bishop Rock
C. Needles D. Bell Rock

537 Which gas has the lowest melting and boiling points?
A. Hydrogen B. Oxygen C. Helium D. Nitrogen

ANSWERS pages 82–83: 524–D. 525–A. 526–A. 527–B. 528–C. 529–A. 530–A. 531–D. 532–B. 533–A. 534–D. 535–A. 536–B. 537–C

---

538 Which river fills the world's largest dam, the Grand Coulee Dam in the USA?
A. Colorado B. Rio Grande
C. Columbia D. Missouri

539 Where would you find Stanley Kent's fibres?
A. Inside a human heart
B. Inside a cricket ball
C. In a tough but light climbing rope
D. In the equipment of a man who ties artificial flies for trout anglers

540 What was the stage name used by Sydney Francis Patrick Chippendall Healey-Kay?
A. Max Miller B. Old Mother Riley
C. Robert Helpmann D. Anton Dolin

541 Which famous American general's middle name was Tecumseh?
A. Patton B. MacArthur C. Bradley D. Sherman

542 What is measured by the Douglas scales, invented in 1921 by Captain H P Douglas of the Royal Navy?
A. The quantity of the rum ration
B. The speed of wind in a ship's sails
C. The smoothness of the sea's surface
D. The weight of large items of cargo

543 Which Victorian artist said, 'If people only knew as much about painting as I do, they would never buy my pictures'?
A. William Frith B. Sir Edwin Landseer

C. Sir John Everett Millais D. William Holman Hunt

544 What can be written down in the Wade-Giles system?
A. The Chinese language, in Western lettering
B. Scoring patterns in basketball
C. Chemical experiments
D. Athletes' movements in throwing events, such as the discus

545 Which country's capital was founded in the early 17th century by a Turkish general, Barkinzade Suleyman Pasha, and was originally called Teheran?
A. Iraq B. Iran C. Albania D. Bulgaria

546 How many days does it take for a million seconds to pass?
A. 81 B. 116 C. 212 D. 581

547 In the 'Eagle' comic, what was the name of Dan Dare's batman?
A. Digby B. Hubert C. George D. Angus

548 Where was the artist Domenicos Theotocopoulos, known as El Greco, born in 1541?
A. Athens B. Corfu C. Crete D. Barcelona

549 Which modern musical instrument was developed from the sackbut?
A. Xylophone B. Trombone
C. French horn D. Oboe

550 Which pop group has made two successful albums with the titles of Marx Brothers films, 'A Night at the Opera' and 'A Day at the Races'?
A. Pink Floyd B. Moody Blues
C. Fleetwood Mac D. Queen

ANSWERS pages 84–85: 538–C. 539–A. 540–D. 541–D. 542–C. 543–B. 544–A. 545–C. 546–B. 547–A. 548–C. 549–B. 550–D.

---

551 In which state of the USA is the Ossining Correctional Facility, formerly called Sing Sing Prison?
A. New York B. Florida
C. Michigan D. California

552 Which famous film star, the son of a judge, wanted to be a cartoonist and trained as one, but couldn't get the work, so became a film extra instead?
A. Clark Gable B. Gary Cooper
C. Henry Fonda D. Charles Boyer

553 When Bette Davis was voted 'Queen of Hollywood' in 1940, who was voted 'King' by the readers of Fortune Magazine?
A. Mickey Rooney B. Clark Gable
C. Errol Flynn D. James Cagney

554 The film 'Lily of the Dust' was remade in 1933 as 'The Song of Songs' and was publicised by nude statues of the star being placed in cinema foyers. Who was the star?
A. Bette Davis B. Marlene Dietrich
C. Ruby Keeler D. Clara Bow

555 During World War One, one Arab leader, Beni Atiyeh, wrote to Feisal of Mecca, 'Send us a lurens and we will blow up trains with it.' What did he mean by a 'lurens'?
A. A leader like Lawrence of Arabia
B. A biplane fitted with bomb racks
C. A motorised Rolls Royce for desert warfare
D. A heavy artillery gun on its own rails

556 What was the cargo of the Mary Celeste on her last fateful voyage in 1872 when all her crew inexplicably vanished?
A. Molasses B. Commercial alcohol
C. Wheat D. Iron ore

557 Which famous novel was originally going to be called 'All's Well That Ends Well'?
A. Treasure Island B. Pride and Prejudice
C. Peyton Place D. War and Peace

558 Which motor-car was the make chosen by each American president from Taft in 1909 to F D Roosevelt in 1945?
A. Chevrolet B. Pierce-Arrow
C. Cadillac D. Lincoln

559 Which one of these fruits will *not* continue to ripen after picking?
A. Pears B. Bananas C. Apricots D. Pineapples

560 Which of these foods have American servicemen voted that they dislike most?
A. Fried parsnips B. Creamed onions
C. Boiled pigs' feet D. Canned figs

561 In the 16th century, what did people refer to as 'mubbleflubbles'?
A. Deep depression, the blues B. Freckles or pimples
C. Unnecessary decorations on clothes D. Silly rumours or lies

562 If you measured a composer's output by the total number of hours it would take to play through all his known work, who wrote the most, about 340 hours in all?
A. Mozart B. Haydn C. Handel D. Beethoven

563 What was the name of the 'Stupid Boy!' character played by Ian Lavender in 'Dad's Army'?
A. Dixon B. West C. Adams D. Pike

ANSWERS pages 86–87: 551–A. 552–B. 553–A. 554–B. 555–A. 556–B. 557–D. 558–B. 559–D. 560–A. 561–A. 562–B. 563–D

---

564 Hamlet, Prince of Denmark, is the longest part in a Shakespeare play, but which of Shakespeare's Kings is given most to say?
A. Henry V B. King Lear
C. Richard II D. Richard III

565 Which later famous actor was Vincent Price's deaf-mute assistant in the 1953 horror film, 'House of Wax', made in 3-D?
A. Jack Nicholson B. Steve McQueen
C. Charles Bronson D. Charlton Heston

566 Which comedian's radio show introduced the character of Whippit Kwick, a cat-burglar?
A. Ted Ray B. Tommy Handley
C. Kenneth Horne D. Charlie Chester

567 In a Thai restaurant, if you ordered Pla tom yam, which of these Thai specialities ought you to get?
A. Spiced fish soup B. Grilled king prawns
C. Tossed salad D. Deep-fried boiled eggs

568 Which country did England once beat at cricket by an innings and 579 runs?
A. South Africa in 1922 B. Australia in 1938
C. Pakistan in 1961 D. West Indies in 1952

569 Before David Moorcroft, who was the last British athlete to hold the world record for the 5000 metres?
A. Gordon Pirie B. Christopher Chataway

C. David Bedford D. Brendan Foster

570 Who says in the Bible, 'I am a brother to dragons, and a companion to owls'?
A. King David B. John the Baptist
C. Ezekiel D. Job

571 What do the British call the chess piece known as a 'fool' or 'fou' by the French?
A. Pawn B. Knight C. Bishop D. Rook

572 What do the Irish Rugby Union call their equivalent of the Barbarians, a team formed from prominent players of several countries?
A. Leprechauns B. Shamrocks
C. Wolfhounds D. Emeralds

573 Late in the 19th century, what was known as 'the navvy's prayer-book'?
A. The magazine 'Titbits'
B. A race-card at a horse-racing meeting
C. A box to hold sandwiches
D. A shovel

574 From which language do we get the slang term 'stir', meaning 'prison'?
A. Gaelic B. Yiddish C. Romany D. Turkish

575 Which of these definitions does not fit the word 'mungo', though the other three do?
A. Reclaimed wool B. A young salmon
C. A garbage-sorter D. A mongoose

576 What is qhythsontyd?
A. An obsolete form of 'Whitsuntide'
B. A fifty-unit note of Albanian currency
C. The Saudi Arabian secret service
D. A completely imaginary word produced by random typing

ANSWERS pages 88–89: 564–D. 565–C. 566–D. 567–A. 568–B. 569–A. 570–D. 571–C. 572–C. 573–D. 574–C. 575–B. 576–A.

---

577 What is a scaldabanco?
A. A slang word for a risk-taker
B. An Icelandic epic poem
C. A fiery preacher or debater
D. A Spanish Punch and Judy show

578 Stigonomancy is a kind of fortune-telling, but what does the fortune-teller consult?
A. Coffee grounds B. Tree bark
C. Orange peel D. The soles of your feet

579 In old English law, what was the custom of thwertnick?
A. Entertaining a sheriff for three nights
B. Holding a mock fight on New Year's Eve
C. Tipping rubbish over minor offenders
D. Making drunks pay fines into the church poor-box

580 What does a noseconologist study?
A. The design of rockets
B. Short intervals of time
C. The use of drugs in sport
D. Hospital administration

581 What does QUTB mean?
A. Queen's Ulster Training Battalion
B. The highest degree of sainthood in Islam
C. Queensland University Translation Bureau
D. A quadruple-strength bacteria-killer

582 Which of these is *not* a hot and dusty wind in the desert or the Mediterranean?

A. Shamal B. Solano C. Simoom D. Shapoo

583 In 1948, which famous poet was discovered not to have paid any income tax for sixteen years?
A. T S Eliot B. Dylan Thomas
C. John Betjeman D. Robert Graves

584 Which film star was awarded his first Oscar in 1972, when he was 83 years old, though he'd earlier been given an honorary Academy Award?
A. George Burns B. Henry Fonda
C. Charlie Chaplin D. James Cagney

585 Which science fiction film had the highest budget, costing 46 million dollars to make?
A. Star Trek B. Star Wars
C. Superman D. The Empire Strikes Back

586 Why was traffic allowed to cross the Severn Bridge free for the first time ever on a day in January 1982?
A. To celebrate the fifteenth anniversary of the bridge opening
B. Snow stopped the toll-collectors getting to work
C. The collecting authority had forgotten to renew their licence
D. The toll collectors were on strike

587 When Mark Thatcher and his co-driver Charlotte Vernay got lost driving through the Sahara, where were they going? Or rather, where did they originally intend to go?
A. Timbuctoo, in Mali B. Ibadan, in Nigeria
C. Dakar, in Senegal D. Accra, in Ghana

588 When the Pope visited Britain in 1982, which Cathedral did he visit first?
A. Canterbury B. Coventry
C. Liverpool D. Westminster

ANSWERS pages 90–91: 577–C. 578–B. 579–A. 580–D. 581–B. 582–D.(Shapoo is a wild mountain sheep from Tibet) 583–B. 584–C. 585–A. 586–B. 587–C. 588–D

---

589 Why did Gloucester County Council refuse to accept an offer of free milk for its schoolchildren in 1982?
A. They objected to the EEC milk regulations
B. They thought the milk would make children fat
C. Teachers refused to organise giving out the milk
D. They couldn't get bottles smaller than one pint

590 What relation is the editor of 'The Times', Charles Douglas-Home, to the former Prime Minister, Sir Alec Douglas-Home?
A. Son B. Grandson
C. Nephew D. No relation at all

591 Which is the only one of these countries to alter its clocks to enjoy Summer Time each year?
A. Japan B. Iceland C. Albania D. Yugoslavia

592 Which former union chief called his autobiography 'Battered Cherub'?
A. Tom Jackson (Post Office)
B. Frank Chapple (Electricians)
C. Joe Gormley (Miners)
D. Bill Sirs (Steel)

593 During the Falklands War, what was the name of Argentina's only aircraft carrier, which stayed in port?
A. The Twenty-first of June
B. The Twenty-ninth of August
C. The Fifteenth of January
D. The Twenty-fifth of May

594 When the Pope left Britain at the end of his 1982 visit, which sports event was taking place on the same day?
A. Wimbledon B. The Derby
C. Henley Regatta D. Test Match

595 What do you have to do well to win the Carl Flesch award?
A. Play a violin B. Arrange flowers
C. Pass Law exams D. Play croquet

596 Britain's new fighter-bomber plane to replace Jaguar and Phantom jets was provisionally called an ACA, meaning what?
A. Advanced Combat Aircraft
B. Active Combat Aircraft
C. Agile Combat Aircraft
D. Armoured Combat Aircraft

597 Who represented the Queen at the Funeral of Princess Grace of Monaco in September 1982?
A. The Prince of Wales B. The Princess of Wales
C. Princess Anne D. Princess Margaret

598 What do Dungeness, Titchwell and Loch of Kinnordy have in common?
A. Nuclear power stations B. RAF bombing ranges
C. Submarine bases D. Bird sanctuaries

599 When Prince Andrew and Koo Stark flew to the West Indies on holiday together, what name did they use to book their plane tickets?
A. Mr & Mrs Cambridge B. Mr & Mrs Oxford
C. Mr & Mrs Stratford D. Mr & Mrs Manchester

600 Where's Dum Dum airport?
A. Shanghai B. Caracas C. Calcutta D. Tokyo

ANSWERS pages 92–93: 589–B. 590–C. 591–A. 592–C. 593–D. 594–B. 595–A. 596–C. 597–B. 598–D. 599–A. 600–C

---

601 Who or what do Spaniards refer to as 'El Gordo' or 'The Fat One'?
A. A famous bull-fighter B. The Christmas lottery
C. Madrid Cathedral D. The late General Franco

602 How did Sue Brown make news in 1981?
A. She was the first test-tube baby
B. She became Secretary of the Water Workers Union
C. She coxed Oxford in the Boat Race
D. She won the Miss England title

603 What's the nickname of the American golfer Craig Stadler
A. Fuzzy B. Walrus C. Flubber D. Dink

604 In the 1982 World Cup finals in Spain, which team had the worst record, scoring only one goal and losing every game it played?
A. Cameroons B. Kuwait C. Algeria D. El Salvador

605 What is Brown Willy?
A. A trout fly B. An off-shore wind in Jamaica
C. The highest point in Cornwall D. A tropical fish

606 In which sport do competitors score points for the speed with which they can dress themselves in full equipment, starting from a kneeling position behind their piled-up gear?
A. Kendo B. Jai-alai C. Aikido D. Bushido

607 In which sport are there American teams called the Detroit Pistons and the Chicago Bulls?

A. Basketball B. Baseball
C. American Football D. Soccer

608 What is called the 'Ras Iechyd-da' in Welsh, or 'Good Health Race'?
A. A nine-day cycle race round Wales
B. A New Year's Eve road race through Mountain Ash
C. A swim across the Bristol Channel
D. The Cardigan Bay marathon road race

609 Who wrote the music for ballets called 'Miracle in the Gorbals' and 'Adam Zero'?
A. Benjamin Britten B. Arthur Bliss
C. Igor Stravinsky D. André Previn

610 Which country's crown jewels include the Great Monomach Cap and a crown made of a cone of gold pieces with a fur edging?
A. Russia B. Sweden C. Norway D. Nepal

611 Who was the first boxer to regain the World Heavyweight Boxing title after losing it?
A. Jack Johnson B. Ingemar Johansson
C. Floyd Patterson D. Muhammad Ali

612 What's the meaning of the word 'Sputnik', used for the Earth's first artificial satellite?
A. Wandering star B. Bright bird
C. New moon D. Fellow traveller

613 What are Portsoken, Vintry and Candlewick?
A. Villages in the 'Watch with Mother' stories for children
B. Electoral wards in the City of London
C. Types of home-woven blankets
D. Varieties of eating apples

ANSWERS pages 94–95: 601–B. 602–C. 603–B. 604–D. 605–C. 606–A. 607–A. 608–A. 609–B. 610–A. 611–C. 612–D. 613–B.

---

614 Which of these is *not* one of the Scilly Islands?
A. St John's B. St Martin's
C. St Agnes D. St Mary's

615 What's a yaffle?
A. A yacht flag B. A complicated knot
C. An antelope D. A woodpecker

616 A turbit is a kind of what?
A. Gerbil B. Pigeon
C. Tropical fish D. Carving in a church

617 Which is the largest in area of these four?
A. Gibraltar B. Vatican City C. Sark D. Monaco

618 Which is the smallest of these islands?
A. Anglesey B. Isle of Man
C. Malta D. Isle of Wight

619 Which Prince was the husband of Queen Anne?
A. Henry B. Edward C. Richard D. George

620 Which widow of an English king was forbidden to remarry by a special Act of Parliament?
A. Catherine of Valois, widow of Henry V
B. Catherine Parr, widow of Henry VIII
C. Henrietta Maria, widow of Charles I
D. Catherine of Braganza, widow of Charles II

621 Where would you find Cassini's Division?

A. In the Great Rift Valley of Africa
B. In the human liver
C. In the rings of Saturn
D. In a mathematical text-book

622 From which other country did the USA buy nearly 30 000 square miles of territory in the Gadsden Purchase of 1853?
A. France B. Russia C. Mexico D. Spain

623 What did Julio Iglesias do before he became a singer?
A. He washed cars in Barcelona
B. He was goalkeeper with Real Madrid
C. He was a cameraman for Spanish television
D. He was a trainee bullfighter in Granada

624 When the fingers are called index, medius, annularis and minimus, what is the thumb called?
A. Tundax B. Carthax C. Dunlex D. Pollex

625 Who was the first British martyr to be made a saint?
A. St Alban B. St Pancras
C. St Edmund D. St Vitus

626 How many litres are there in a hectolitre?
A. 10 B. 100
C. 1 000 D. None – a hectolitre is a medical instrument

627 Which of these people didn't appear on the cover of the Beatles record, 'Sgt Pepper's Lonely Hearts Club Band'?
A. Queen Victoria B. Oscar Wilde
C. Albert Einstein D. Dylan Thomas

628 What was the main invention of the novelist Anthony Trollope?
A. Carbon paper B. Stamp machines
C. Pillar boxes D. Egg-timers

ANSWERS pages 96–97: 614–A. 615–D. 616–B. 617–A. 618–C. 619–D. 620–A. 621–C. 622–C. 623–B. 624–D. 625–A. 626–B. 627–A. 628–C.

---

629 In the oil industry, how many American gallons are there in a barrel?
A. 20 B. 28 C. 35 D. 42

630 Who, or what, is Raks Sharki?
A. The original Middle East name for belly-dancing
B. A notorious double agent
C. A small purple-coloured flower, not unlike a tulip
D. A submission hold in judo that is now banned

631 Which US state has as its motto, 'Manly deeds, womanly words'?
A. Alaska B. Maryland
C. North Carolina
D. Kentucky

632 In which of these novels does Richard Hannay feature?
A. Thirty-nine Steps B. Island of Sheep
C. Three Hostages D. Greenmantle

633 Which sign of the Zodiac features a goat?
A. Cancer B. Capricorn C. Pisces D. Sagittarius

634 In which imaginary land do geese fly through the air ready-roasted?
A. Cockaigne B. Utopia
C. Never Never Land D. Erewhon

635 Why was Vincent Lunardi famous?
A. As an early surgeon
B. As an early balloonist

C. As the inventor of the shooting stick
D. As the inventor of the crash helmet

636 What name did actors David Carradine and Barbara Hershey give to their son, born in 1974?
A. Dove B. Free C. Reagan D. Jip

637 In 1941, which country annexed Lithuania?
A. Germany B. Russia C. Italy D. Spain

638 How many years BC did the last glaciers disappear from Britain?
A. 2 000 B. 8 000 C. 20 000 D. 50 000

639 What is Tony Meo's game?
A. Darts B. Cricket C. Snooker D. Rugby

640 What is the temperature on the planet Venus?
A. −400°F B. 0°F C. 400°F D. 800°F

641 What was odd about the cricket match between Gondwanaland Occasionals and Beardmore Casuals played in January 1985?
A. Play was stopped by an invasion of ostriches
B. Food poisoning incapacitated the entire fielding side
C. It was played about 400 miles away from the South Pole, the furthest south any cricket match has been played on record
D. Four batsmen collapsed, suffering from sunstroke – the temperature was 115°F in the shade

642 When the first Woolworth store opened in 1879, what was the maximum cost of any item on sale?
A. 5 cents B. 10 cents C. 25 cents D. One dollar

643 From which language does the word 'tycoon' come?
A. English B. Turkish C. Greek D. Chinese

ANSWERS pages 98–99: 629–D. 630–A. 631–B. 632–A,B,C,D.(Yes, all of them) 633–B. 634–A. 635–B. 636–B. 637–B. 638–B. 639–C. 640–D. 641–C. 642–A. 643–D

---

644 Which was the first horse to win the Grand National three times?
A. Reynoldstown B. The Colonel
C. Red Rum D. Crisp

645 In the Bible, who was accused of strangling her 7 husbands?
A. Salome B. Esther C. Ruth D. Sarah

646 In the Bible, through what type of burning bush did God speak to Moses?
A. A gooseberry bush B. A blackberry bush
C. A holly bush D. The Bible doesn't specify

647 In 'Who's Who' entrants give their recreation. Who changed it, over the years, no fewer than 32 times? (Ranging from 'Reading "Who's Who"' to 'Getting used to retirement.')
A. Lord Wilson B. Lord Stockton
C. Lord Wolfenden D. Lord Boothby

648 Which drink was originally labelled the 'Esteemed Brain Tonic and Intellectual Beverage'?
A. Pepsi-Cola B. 7 Up C. Coca-Cola D. Sarsaparilla

649 What temperature is absolute zero?
A. −107.42°F B. −273.16°F
C. −459.69°F D. −1011.35°F

650 What is the colour of Mr Spock's blood, of 'Star Trek' fame?

A. Red B. Blue C. Green D. Yellow

651 Which country was the first to give women the right to vote?
A. USA B. Britain C. Australia D. New Zealand

652 Where did Queen Victoria die?
A. Sandringham B. Osborne House
C. Buckingham Palace D. Gleneagles

653 What was the first product advertised on TV in Britain?
A. Pears Soap B. Gibb's SR Toothpaste
C. Kit Kat D. Bournvita

654 What is a jansky?
A. An Americanism for a very young pop singer
B. An early gas-filled balloon
C. The unit of depth, for divers only using scuba equipment
D. A measurement of radio signals from outer space

655 Which element was discovered by Joseph Priestley?
A. Oxygen B. Hydrogen C. Nitrogen D. Sulphur

656 Whose hitherto unknown opera was discovered in a London basement in 1984?
A. Rossini B. Donizetti C. Puccini D. Haydn

657 In which month is the US festival of Thanksgiving celebrated?
A. September B. October
C. November D. December

658 In which year were nylon stockings first made?
A. 1917 B. 1927 C. 1937 D.1947

ANSWERS pages 100–101: 644–C. 645–D. 646–D. 647–C. 648–C. 649–C. 650–C. 651–D. 652–B. 653–B. 654–D. 655–A. 656–B. 657–C. 658–C

---

659 In the USA, which are the only two states in which gambling casinos are legal?
A. Nevada and New York
B. Nevada and New Jersey
C. Nevada and Montana
D. Nevada and Arizona

660 In the 1950s, which dress designer originated the sack?
A. Christian Dior B. Yves St Laurent
C. Jean Rook D. Balenciaga

661 Which ex-Wimbledon tennis champion was defeated 6–4, 6–3, 6–3 by Billie Jean King at the Houston Astrodome in 1973?
A. Bill Tilden B. Bobby Riggs
C. Jack Kramer D. Lew Hoad

662 Who founded the Quakers?
A. William Booth B. George Fox
C. William Pitt the younger D. Elizabeth Fry

663 On which LP cover did John Lennon and Yoko Ono appear nude?
A. Two Virgins B. Shaved Fish
C. Mind Games D. Double Fantasy

664 Who, in 1973 said, 'I would not be candid if I did not admit that this has not been an easy year in some respects'?
A. Sebastian Coe B. Geoffrey Boycott
C. Richard Nixon D. Ronnie Kray

665 What did Silas Noble and James P Cooley invent?
A. The toothpick B. Elastic

C. Cellophane D. The shopping trolley

666 In which part of the body is insulin manufactured?
A. The kidneys B. The pancreas
C. The liver D. The stomach

667 Which great cricketer also once held the world long jump record?
A. C B Fry B. Colin Cowdrey
C. Jack Hobbs D. W G Grace

668 With what subject does the American magazine 'Bondage' deal?
A. Quality paper, and printing techniques
B. Sexual perversions
C. Leather straps and ski bindings
D. James Bond

669 How long does the planet Pluto take to complete its orbit of the sun?
A. 31 Earth years B. 62 Earth years
C. 124 Earth years D. 248 Earth years

670 To prevent which illness would you be given Pertussis vaccine?
A. Measles B. German Measles
C. Whooping Cough D. Scarlet Fever

671 Which was the Beatles' first Number One hit in the USA?
A. 'Love Me Do' B. 'Eleanor Rigby'
C. 'I Want to Hold your Hand' D. 'Yellow Submarine'

672 What colour shoes does Gary Player wear when playing competitive golf?
A. White B. Blue C. Brown D. Black

ANSWERS pages 102–103: 659–B. 660–A. 661–B. 662–B. 663–A. 664–C. 665–A. 666–B. 667–A. 668–D. 669–D. 670–C. 671–C. 672–D.

---

673 What was Jayne Mansfield's favourite colour – both her house and car were this colour?
A. Pink B. White C. Black D. Turquoise

674 In what were the first baked beans served?
A. Tomato sauce B. Black treacle
C. Redcurrant jelly D. Golden Syrup

675 Big Brother was watching us in 1984. According to whom?
A. J B Priestley B. Aldous Huxley
C. George Orwell D. Graham Greene

676 At what sport do 'The Tiger Top Tuskers' and 'The Pan Am Jumbos' compete?
A. Elephant Polo (4 elephants a side, each with mahout, player and a man at the back)
B. Baseball
C. Hawaiian Football
D. Hockey (New Zealand code)

677 How many legs has a wayzgoose?
A. None B. 2
C. 4 D. 6

678 Who was the oldest footballer to make an England debut?
A. Leslie Compton B. Stanley Matthews
C. Jimmy Greaves D. Gordon Banks

679 Where is Kai Tak airport?
A. Hong Kong B. China C. Korea D. Japan

680 Who was Britain's first Prime Minister in 1721?

A. Robert Walpole B. William Pitt Senior
C. Lord Salisbury D. Andrew Jackson

681 Who invented the first diesel engine?
A. Carl Benz B. Rudolf Diesel
C. Gottlieb Daimler D. Charles Rolls

682 Where was Brighthelmstone?
A. Brighton
B. Westminster Abbey
C. The start of Hadrian's Wall
D. The end of Offa's Dyke

683 By whom was Bradley J Baxter of Wichita, Kansas, strangled?
A. His pet orang-utan
B. A henchman of Al Capone
C. His local piano tuner, when he suggested to him that he had lowered the pitch of the piano
D. His wife's lover's brother

684 Everyone knows what a jay-walker is, but why is he so called?
A. The very first recorded pedestrian fatality in a car accident was Adolphus S Jay
B. 'Jay' is American slang for a clumsy or careless person
C. The jay is an awkward bird that often does foolish things, such as walk across a busy road
D. It derives from an old Urdu word implying a desire to commit suicide

685 What is 'Ondine's Curse'?
A. A curse on all would-be Shakespearian actors
B. The curse of witches about to be burnt at the stake
C. A rare breathing disease where the sufferer cannot breathe while asleep
D. The complaint of a bridge player who holds a long succession of appalling hands

ANSWERS pages 104–105: 673–A. 674–B. 675–C. 676–A. 677–A.(It is a printers' annual picnic.) 678–A.(He was 38) 679–A. 680–A. 681–B. 682–A.(It was the old name of the town) 683–A. 684–B. 685–C

---

686 Inventor Reuben Tice died when the invention on which he was working blew up. What was he trying to create?
A. An oven that became a refrigerator at the turn of a switch
B. A device to fit to parking meters so that they automatically reset themselves as the time actually paid for ran out
C. A safe blower for safe-blowers
D. A machine to take the wrinkles out of prunes

687 What institution did Mrs Tealby found in 1871?
A. Covent Garden Market
B. Wigmore Hall for musicians to give their public recitals
C. The Reading Room at the British Museum
D. Battersea Dogs' Home

688 In which European country is the National Orchestra larger than the army?
A. Monaco B. France C. Andorra D. Portugal

689 Before becoming an actor, what was Burt Lancaster's profession?
A. Docker B. Policeman
C. Circus acrobat D. Schoolteacher

690 Who is, or was, Edmond Dantes?
A. Robespierre
B. The Count of Monte Cristo
C. The prosecutor in the De Lorean case
D. The short-lived 'Breakfast Time' TV news presenter

691 Who shared the Oscar for Best Actress with Katharine Hepburn in 1968?
A. Jane Wyman B. Elizabeth Taylor
C. Anne Bancroft D. Barbra Streisand

692 When did BP first strike oil in the North Sea?
A. 1950 B. 1960 C. 1965 D. 1975

693 Which of the following research establishments never existed?
A. The Cereals Research station at St Albans
B. The Printing, Paper and Packaging Research Association at Leatherhead.
C. The National College of Food Technology at Weybridge
D. The Sahara Forestry Commission at Herne Bay

694 Why are camel-hair brushes so called?
A. Because Mr Camel invented them
B. Because they are made of camel hair
C. Because the first ones were camel coloured
D. For no very good reason

695 What was special about the 1978–79 Scottish cup between Inverness Thistle and Falkirk?
A. It was postponed 29 times
B. The visiting team were taken to the wrong ground 132 miles away
C. There was the longest recorded stoppage for crowd trouble
D. There were more police present than spectators

696 Which was the first nation ever to resign from the United Nations
A. China B. USSR C. Pakistan D. Indonesia

697 In which country was Omar Sharif born?
A. Jordan B. Egypt C. France D. Iran

ANSWERS pages 106–107: 686–D. 687–D. 688–A. 689–C. 690–B. 691–D. 692–C. 693–D. 694–A. 695–A. 696–D. 697–B

---

698 Marc Quinquandon was a world champion. At what?
A. Lying on a bed of nails
B. Snail-eating
C. Stripping pine doors
D. Pulling ugly faces

699 Who was the first American astronaut to go into space twice?
A. John Young B. John Glenn
C. Neil Armstrong D. Michael Collins

700 Where did Hermann Goering hide the poison with which he committed suicide in 1946?
A. In his hair B. In a false tooth
C. Under a false navel D. In a button on his trousers

701 Who is, or was, Ruth Draper?
A. The only woman in Sherlock Holmes's life
B. A stage star famous for her solo performances
C. A celebrated poisoner, brought to trial in 1885
D. The first woman to climb the Matterhorn

702 'Tailgating' is an American expression. What does it mean?
A. Selling things from the boot of your car at a one-day open air market
B. Pursuing young females in a 'singles bar'
C. Picnicking in the car before a big sports event
D. Reversing a heavy truck into security defences as a prelude to a smash and grab raid

703 How did singer Sebastiano Maldi die, in 1819?
A. He was killed when a pressure cooker, newly invented, blew up near him
B. A fly flew into his throat when he was singing in Paris, and he choked
C. He fell off the stage into the orchestra pit during rehearsal and died from his injuries
D. He was accidentally knifed by an overenthusiastic baritone

704 Who won Britain's first ever Winter Olympics Gold Medal
A. M J Altwegg B. A Nash and R Dixon
C. J Curry D. P Fleming

705 What shook up Britain on July 19, 1984?
A. The price of British Telecom's shares when they were first quoted on the stock exchange
B. The massive fire at York Minster
C. The announcement of Clive Sinclair's new electric vehicle
D. Britain's biggest earthquake for 100 years

706 Name Chuck Campbell's dummy in 'Soap'.
A. Ben B. Bert C. Jodie D. Bob

707 In which 1883 novel does the Admiral Benbow Inn feature?
A. Treasure Island B. Pickwick Papers
C. David Copperfield D. Kidnapped

708 Which first division football club once supplied seven players for an England team?
A. Liverpool B. Arsenal
C. Manchester United D. Tottenham Hotspur

709 To date, who was the heaviest world boxing champion?
A. Muhammad Ali B. Max Baer
C. Rocky Marciano D. Primo Carnera

ANSWERS pages 108–109: 698–B. 699–A. 700–C. 701–B. 702–C. 703–A. 704–A. 705–D. 706–D. 707–A. 708–B. 709–D.

---

710 What is 'knockback'?
A. A tennis player simply blocking a powerful shot by his opponent, without attempting a recognised stroke
B. A parole board refusing a prisoner's request for release
C. A blow delivered with the back of the hand in all-in wrestling
D. A recurrent but intermittent fault in hi-fi equipment

711 Who was known as 'America's Sweetheart'?
A. Mary Pickford B. Shirley Temple
C. Jane Wyman D. Sophie Tucker

712 Who or what are Sydenham Damerel, Curry Mallet and Mary Tavy?
A. Varieties of crocus
B. Characters in two of Anthony Trollope's novels
C. Devon villages
D. The assumed names of the brothers and sisters of Daniel Defoe

713 Which partner of Lee Majors was Farrah Fawcett?
A. 1st wife B. 2nd wife C. 3rd wife D. 4th wife

714 In the Bible, what animal did Joseph's brothers kill in order to smear his coat with blood?
A. A bull B. A cow C. A goat D. A sheep

715 In which century were houses first numbered in London?
A. 15th Century B. 16th Century
C. 17th Century D. 18th Century

716 Which is the world's busiest airport?
A. John F Kennedy (New York) B. Heathrow (London)
C. Zurich (Switzerland) D. O'Hare (Chicago)

717 Name the vehicle in which Irwin and Scott took their first ever drive – on the moon.
A. Moon Buggy B. Lunar Runabout
C. Moon Moke D. Lunar Roving Vehicle

718 What is Rumford's Soup?
A. A recipe for a cheap soup suggested by Count von. Rumford
B. A constellation of stars in the farthest part of the Milky Way
C. A head-lock in Graeco-Roman wrestling
D. The spawn of frogs from which tadpoles hatch

719 Who was the very first winner of BBC TV's Mastermind?
A. Sir David Hunt B. Nancy Wilkinson
C. Patricia Owen D. Elizabeth Horrocks

720 What is a doppelganger?
A. A Wagnerian bass singer
B. Someone's double
C. A labourer in one of the Dutch doppels
D. The German equivalent of a punk singer

721 Which game begins with a bully-off?
A. Lacrosse B. Hockey
C. Netball D. Water Polo

722 Which scientist discovered the most elements?
A. Sir Isaac Newton B. Charles Darwin
C. Galileo D. Sir Humphrey Davy

723 What was the former name of The People's Republic of Kampuchea?
A. North Vietnam B. South Vietnam
C. Siam D. Cambodia

ANSWERS pages 110–111: 710–B. 711–A. 712–C. 713–B. 714–C. 715–D. 716–D. 717–D. 718–A. 719–B. 720–B. 721–B. 722–D. 723–D.

---

724 Who was Charles Peace (1832-1879)?
A. The inventor of deep-freezing
B. A notorious criminal
C. The first man to run a mile in under 4 minutes 30 seconds
D. The Englishman who is reputed to have invented skiing

725 Approximately how many people died in the 1921–22 Russian famine?
A. A million B. 3 million C. 5 million D. 10 million

726 In the USA, what percentage of homes has at least one TV set?
A. 68% B. 78% C. 88% D. 98%

727 Who attempted to invade Ireland in December 1796?
A. The Scots B. The French
c. The Dutch d. The Germans

728 Who founded the Norwich School of Painting?
A. Sir Joshua Reynolds B. John Constable
C. James Whistler D. John Crome

729 In snooker, how many points is the brown ball worth?
A. 2 B. 3 C. 4 D. 5

730 What was the Bionic dog in 'The Six Million Dollar Man' named?
A. Fred B. Jim C. Fluke D. Max.

731 Which TV cop does Erik Estrada play?
A. Dan August in 'Dan August'
B. Andy Renko in 'Hill Street Blues'
C. Frank 'Ponch' Poncherello in 'Chips'
D. Eliot Ness in 'The Untouchables'

732 What is a snood?
A. A South African fish B. A hair net
C. A sign of ridicule D. A meeting of church dignitaries

733 The Six Million Dollar Man was critically injured whilst testing which type of spacecraft?
A. A space shuttle B. A planet probe
C. A recovery unit D. A moon landing craft

734 Frank Herbert's science fiction book 'Dune' has sold over 10 million copies. But how many times was it rejected before a publisher agreed to give it a go?
A. The first one to whom it was shown took it.
B. 8 C. 13 D. 31

735. What is the Chinese restaurant syndrome?
A. A set of symptoms attributed to the consumption of too much monosodium glutamate
B. A hatred of soft Oriental music
C. A hatred of any Oriental mannerisms
D. The humorous name applied to the fashion of wearing fur caps in Tashkent.

736 Which river gave rise to the saying 'To sell down the river'?
A. Mississippi B. Nile C. Amazon D. Thames

737 The opera 'Samson and Delilah' was written by which composer?
A. Saint-Saens B. Mendelssohn
C. Rossini D. Verdi

ANSWERS pages 112–113: 724–B. 725–C. 726–D. 727–B. 728–D. 729–C. 730–D. 731–C. 732–B. 733–D. 734–C. 735–A. 736–A. 737–A.

---

738 How did the phrase 'the real McCoy' originate?
A. After Al McCoy won the middleweight boxing championship in 1914, many boxers changed their names to McCoy to try to pass themselves off as the champ. So Al advertised himself as 'the real McCoy' and the name stuck
B. After Rob McCoy, the head of the McCoy clan was wounded, believed dead, in a clan clash in Scotland, the rest of the clan fled and there were arguments as to who should be the new chief. Then Rob McCoy returned unexpectedly and ended the power struggle
C. It referred to the legal battle around the 1850s as to who was the proper heir to the McCoy property
D. It related to the use of a decoy, the original being the real McCoy

739 Who was the last monarch to enter the House of Commons?
A. Charles I B. Henry VIII
C. Elizabeth I D. Elizabeth II

740 Chess is a sedate game, but what did the Danish grandmaster Bent Larsen complain about at the Hastings tournament a decade ago?
A. The snoring of his opponent
B. The volume of the applause
C. The caperings of a pantomime horse on the floor above
D. Being woken before dawn every day by passing seagulls

741 What did English clergyman William Oughtred invent?
A. The slide rule B. The stethoscope
C. The baby-walker D. The electronic organ

742 What is a herringbone-hop?
A. A square dance
B. A technique used in skiing
C. A fishing fly
D. A jump used in squash as a last resort to avoid a dangerous collision

743 Who was the last British king who personally led his army into battle, in 1743?
A. George I B. George II C. George III D. Henry II

744 King Louis XVI of France passed a law making it illegal to own
A. A handkerchief less than 12cm square?
B. A handkerchief of any shape other than square?
C. A circular handkerchief?
D. A red handkerchief?

745 In which year was flogging as a punishment abolished in the British Navy?
A. 1781 B. 1831 C. 1881 D. 1931

746 If you have two pairs of roller-skates, a skateboard, a tricycle, a motor-bike and a camel, how many wheels have you?
A. 17 B. 21 C. 23 D. 25

747 From which date each year can Beaujolais Nouveau be sold?
A. September 15 B. October 15
C. November 15 D. December 15

748 On which British banknote does Sir Christopher Wren appear?
A. £5 B. £10 C. £20 D. £50

ANSWERS pages 114–115: 738–A. 739–A. 740–C. 741–A. 742–B. 743–B. 744–B. 745–C. 746–D. 747–C. 748–D.

---

749 Who was the first to get drunk in the Bible?
A. Noah – after planting the first vineyard after the flood
B. Adam – after being despatched from the Garden of Eden
C. David – after killing Goliath
D. Solomon – after deciding the rightful owner of the baby

750 To whom have Elizabeth Taylor and Debbie Reynolds both been married?
A. Eddie Fisher B. Richard Burton
C. Mike Todd D. Roger Vadim

751 What was Charles Walker's claim to fame in 1984?
A. He was the first fare-paying passenger in space
B. He was Britain's first surrogate father
C. He won the competition for the ball used in the FA Cup Final
D. He beat Eric Bristow at darts

752 How old was Henry VI when be became King of England?
A. Under a year B. 6 years C. 36 years D. 76 years

753 In which US state is Harvard University?
A. Massachusetts B. New York
C. Ohio D. Washington

754 Which US city is nicknamed Motown?
A. Chicago B. San Francisco
C. Detroit D. Nashville

755 How often is Halley's Comet seen from earth?

A. Twice each year B. Every second year
C. Once every 22 years D. Once every 76 years

756 Who was the first non-American to win the world heavyweight boxing championship?
A. Tommy Burns (Canada)
B. Robert Fitzsimmons (England)
C. Max Schmeling (Germany)
D. Max Baer (Germany)

757 Which famous film star in his early career earned money by trying out 'Beat The Clock' stunts before they were used by contestants on TV?
A. James Mason B. James Dean
C. James Cagney D. James Garner

758 Of which two metals is bronze an alloy?
A. Copper and tin B. Copper and iron
C. Iron and tin D. Tin and Aluminium

759 The first plague of the Black Death left two European regions least affected. Which were they?
A. Bulgaria and Poland
B. Poland and the Pyrenees
C. The Pyrenees and Germany
D. Germany and The Alps

760 In Greek mythology, whom did Zeus, in the form of a bull, court?
A. Diana B. Ariadne C. Persephone D. Europa

761 In which Shakespearian play does one part have the greatest number of lines?
A. Hamlet in 'Hamlet'
B. Richard II in 'Richard II'
C. Othello in 'Othello'
D. Antony in 'Antony and Cleopatra'

762 Which vegetable is used in a dish described as Lyonnaise?
A. Potato B. Swede C. Onion D. Leek

ANSWERS pages 116–117: 749–A. 750–A. 751–A. 752–A. 753–A. 754–C. 755–D. 756–B. 757–B. 758–A. 759–B. 760–D. 761–A. 762–C.

---

763 A laundry bill dated 1787 was sold at an auction. How much did it fetch?
A. 650 dollars B. 1 100 dollars
C. 2 200 dollars D. 4 400 dollars

764 Which late night TV series invariably begins, 'There's nothing wrong with your TV set. We are controlling the vertical . . .'?
A. 'The Twilight Zone' B. 'The Outer Limits'
C. 'Battlestar Galactica' D. 'The Naked City'

765 What did Fred Morrison perfect?
A. The flush loo B. The waste disposal unit
C. The frisbee D. Backgammon

766 Where are the Elgin Marbles?
A. The Parthenon B. The British Museum
C. The Colosseum, Rome D. The Louvre, Paris

767 What is the official residence of the Lord Mayor of London?
A. Somerset House B. Mansion House
C. Guildhall D. St James's Palace

768 Whose catchphrase is, 'I'm in charge'?
A. Larry Grayson B. Bob Monkhouse
C. Bruce Forsyth D. Bamber Gascoigne

769 Off which islands did a British fleet destroy Vice-Admiral Maximilian Von Spee's fleet during World War One?
A. Falkland Islands B. Canary Islands
C. Greek Islands D. Hebridean Islands

770 Fred Perry was effectively Amateur World Tennis Champion in the mid 1930s, having won the Wimbledon singles titles in 1934, 1935 and 1936. At which other game had he been the world champion in the previous decade?
A. Real Tennis B. Table Tennis C. Squash D. Fives

771 How many ships were there in the Spanish Armada that England defeated in 1588?
A. 60 B. 120 C. 240 D. 480

772 Which area of Canada is an island in the St Lawrence river?
A. Ottawa B. Ontario C. Montreal D. Quebec

773 Who broke the world record for books written in one year, by having 21 published in 1976?
A. John Creasey B. Enid Blyton
C. Agatha Christie D. Barbara Cartland

774 In which year did Adolf Hilter become Chancellor of Germany?
A. 1923 B. 1929 C. 1933 D. 1937

775 Name Captain Flint's pirate ship in Treasure Island.
A. Painted Lady B. Sea Hawk
C. Walrus D. Dragon

776 Every Good Boy Deserves Fruit. For what is this a recognised mnemonic?
A. The Great Lakes
B. The principle characters of 'Gone with the Wind'
C. The five lines of the treble musical stave
D. The Plantagenet Kings of England

777 What is performed or shown in the Queen Elizabeth Hall?
A. Films B. Plays C. Mimes D. Concerts

ANSWERS pages 118–119: 763–B. 764–B. 765–C. 766–B. 767–B. 768–C. 769–A. 770–B. 771–B. 772–C. 773–D. 774–C. 775–C. 776–C. 777–D.

---

778 What distinguishes a Welsh harp from other types?
A. It is particularly large and triple stringed
B. It is small and has no pedals
C. It is tuned to the pentatonic scale
D. Nothing very much

779 Who played General George Custer in 'Santa Fé Trail'?
A. Clint Eastwood B. Dirk Bogarde
C. John Wayne D. Ronald Reagan

780 Who was known as The Sage of Chelsea?
A. Hans Sloane B. Thomas Carlyle
C. Capability Brown D. Dr Johnson

781 What is the nickname given to the scientist Edward Teller?
A. Father of the H-Bomb B. The Plutonium Blond
C. The Apple Man D. The Big Banger

782 Whose ghost reputedly returns to Blickling Hall in Norfolk on May 19 each year, sitting in a coach drawn by four headless horses and driven by a headless coachman, carrying her own head on her knees?
A. Catherine Howard B. Joan of Arc
C. Anne Boleyn D. Mary, Queen of Scots

783 Of which principality is Vaduz the capital?
A. Bolivia B. Peru C. Andorra D. Liechtenstein

784 For which naval rank is a 'snotty' slang?

A. Midshipman B. Chief Engineer
C. Second Officer D. Captain

785 On which children's TV show do The Cookie Monster, Ernie and Big Bird feature?
A. 'Sesame Street' B. 'The Muppets'
C. 'The Moomins' D. 'Jackanory'

786 Consumption is the old name for which disease?
A. Cancer B. Tuberculosis
C. Legionnaires Disease D. Pneumonia

787 Which British Monarch died in 1952?
A. Edward VII B. Edward VIII
C. George V D. George VI

788 For what do the letters e g stand?
A. Exempli gratia B. Exaltus gratia
C. Each good D. Ex genus

789 Simonstown is a major naval base in which country?
A. South Africa B. Zimbabwe C. Malta D. Jamaica

790 In 1896, how many cars were there in the USA?
A. 4 B. 400 C. 4,000 D. 40 0000

791 Of what curious battle tactic was Alexander the Great the instigator?
A. Having his forces cut their hair and beards short, so that the enemy could not grab them
B. Chopping off the manes and tails of horses so that the enemy could not catch hold of there
C. Having his troops in groups of 100, under one leader, then subdivided into tens under a lower level leader
D. Giving presents of elephants to his enemies to slow them down

ANSWERS pages 120–121: 778–A. 779–D. 780–B. 781–A. 782–C. 783–D. 784–A. 785–A. 786–B. 787–D. 788–A. 789–A. 790–A. 791–A.

---

792 Which boxer's real name was Walker Smith?
A. Joe Louis B. Sonny Liston
C. Sugar Ray Robinson D. Archie Moore

793 Remington and Sons were the first company to manufacture typewriters. Previously, what did they make?
A. Sewing machines B. Dustbins
C. Guns D. Printing machines

794 What is Yom Kippur?
A. The Jewish New Year
B. The Jewish Day of Atonement
C. The Jewish Harvest Festival
D. The Jewish Festival of Lights

795 How old was Mozart when he composed the opera 'Bastien and Bastienne'?
A. 6 B. 12 C. 18 D. 24

796 In music key signatures, which is the first flat?
A. A B. B C. C D. D

797 Mork came from Ork, but where did he live on Earth?
A. Boulder, Colorado B. Denver
C. Kansas City D. Austin, Texas

798 'Amahl and the Night Visitors', first performed on Christmas Eve 1951 was written for what medium?
A. Television

B. Coventry Cathedral
C. The Promenade Concerts
D. Glyndebourne Opera

799 What is the harmattan?
A. A wind
B. A current
C. An early form of the Icelandic Parliament
D. Part of the Pacific Ocean

800 Phil Spector wrote a hit featuring words from his father's tombstone: 'To Know Him Is to Love Him'. Who first recorded it?
A. The Teddy Bears B. The Monkees
C. The Animals D. The Crickets

801 Which was the first Sherlock Holmes film to star Basil Rathbone and Nigel Bruce?
A. 'A Study in Scarlet'
B. 'The Sign of Four'
C. 'The Four Just Men'
D. 'The Hound of the Baskervilles'

802 Swords, coins, clubs and chalices were the 15th-century forerunner of what?
A. Clubs, diamonds, hearts and spades – thc four suits on modern playing cards
B. The basis of Britain's pre-decimal currency
C. Loosely, on what our present day weights and measures system is based
D. Modern heraldry

803 How were Genghis and Kublai Khan related?
A. Kublai was Genghis's son
B. Kublai was Genghis's grandson
C. They were brothers
D. They weren't related

ANSWERS pages 122–123: 792–C. 793–C. 794–B. 795–B. 796–B. 797–A. 798–A. 799–A. 800–A. 801–D. 802–A. 803–B.

---

804 Which famous annual event takes place at Olney in Buckinghamshire?
A. The Pancake Race
B. The World Conker Championships
C. The World Tiddlywinks Championships
D. The Dwyle Flonking Championships of Britain

805 On average, what proportion of people are left-handed?
A. One in 3 B. One in 6
C. One in 10 D. One in 20

806 In 'Star Trek' what was Scotty's first name?
A. Ian B. Montgomery C. Bruce D. McTavish

807 King Louis XIV of France – the Sun King – popularised the game of billiards, which he played constantly on doctor's orders. Why was this?
A. It was the only way that they could persuade him to take exercise
B. They felt that the stretching and bending involved would help his constantly upset tum
C. Because it kept him away from the fleshpots
D. Because he was such a poor player that the side bets wagered were a good source of extra income

808 Which authority or authorities did the GLC replace?
A. London County Council and Middlesex CC
B. LCC and Surrey CC
C. LCC
D. LCC, MCC and SCC

809 In Australia there are approximately 13 million people. How many sheep are there?
A. 13 million B. 82 million
C. 104 million D. 145 million

810 Which rock and roll singer had the surname of Penniman?
A. Bill Haley B. Fats Domino
C. Little Richard D. Chubby Checker

811 In which Belgian town is the Menin Gate?
A. Brussels B. Ypres C. Luge D. Antwerp

812 Susannah Wedgwood, the eldest daughter of Josiah Wedgwood, founder of the style of pottery still bearing his name had a famous son. Who was he?
A. Charles Darwin B. Charles Dickens
C. Thomas Edison D. Edgar Allan Poe

813 How old was Billy the Kid when he was shot dead?
A. 21 B.25 C. 31 D. 35

814 As what were the original singing trio of Bing Crosby, Harry Barris and Al Rinker known?
A. The Songbirds B. The Rhythm Boys
C. The Singing Minstrels D. Songsters Three

815 Which was the second book in the trilogy 'The Hitchhiker's Guide to the Galaxy'?
A. 'The Restaurant at the End of the Universe'
B. 'The Shop on the Fourth Star on the Left, Down the Milky Way'
C. 'So Long, and Thanks for All the Fish'
D. 'The Shuttle on Mars to the Freeway on Pluto'

816 Of which Canadian province is Winnipeg the capital?
A. Ontario B. Manitoba
C. Saskatchewan D. Quebec

ANSWERS pages 124–125: 804–A. 805–B. 806–B. 807–B. 808–A. 809–D. 810–C. 811–B. 812–A. 813–A. 814–B. 815–A. 816–B.

---

817 Navigators of British and American bomber planes were given a new tool in 1944 that helped them considerably in their fight against the enemy. What was it?
A. Non-magnetic compasses
B. Special telescopic lenses to pinpoint the target with much greater accuracy.
C. Battery-operated calculators
D. Ballpoint pens, which worked without leaking or drying up at high altitude

818 What is a fogou?
A. An underground, stone-lined passage of the Iron Age, found in Cornwall, the use of which is uncertain
B. The brand name for the latest design in fog lamps
C. An old name for an animal, a cross between a fox and a dog
D. A new slang expression, not yet included in dictionaries, but rapidly gaining vogue, for a particular kind of pipe used for smoking unusual mixtures

819 Which fur is called after a Russian city?
A. Mink B. Sable C. Astrakhan D. Nutria

820 Who wrote, 'A rose is a rose is a rose is a rose'?
A. Gertrude Lawrence B. Gertrude Stein
C. John Steinbeck D. Anonymous

821 How many balls are used in pool, apart from the cue ball?
A. 3 B. 9 C. 15 D. 21

822 Of which country is Serbia now part?
A. Bulgaria B. Yugoslavia
C. Romania D. East Germany

823 'Wilhelm Tell' was the last complete play of which famous playwright?
A. Marlowe B. Shakespeare C. Schiller D. Goethe

824 The Barclay, The Connaught and Claridges are subsidiaries of which other famous hotel?
A. The Ritz B. The Savoy
C. The Dorchester D. The Cumberland

825 In the theatre, what is the meaning of the phrase, 'Paper the house'?
A. Give away complimentary tickets B. Invite celebrities
C. Invite the press and other media D. Redecorate

826 Which Irish town is famed for glass?
A. Donegal B. Limerick C. Waterford D. Cork

827 By what name was Tasmania previously known?
A. Van Diemen's Land B. Cook's Land
C. Vespucci D. West Zealand

828 How many faces has an icosahedron?
A. 16 B. 20 C. 24 D. 28

829 At the 1964 Tokyo Olympics, Britain won both the men's and women's Gold Medals at which athletics event?
A. Long Jump B. 800m
C. High Jump D. 400m hurdles

830 Who rode Mill Reef to victory in the 1971 Derby and Prix de L'Arc de Triomphe?
A. Geoff Lewis B. Lester Piggott
C. Scobie Breasley D. Steve Cauthen

ANSWERS pages 126–127: 817–D. 818–A. 819–C. 820–B. 821–C. 822–B. 823–C. 824–B. 825–A. 826–C. 827–A. 828–B. 829–A. 830–A.

---

831 Which Pulitzer prize winner wrote the novel on which the musical 'South Pacific' was based?
A. James Michener B. Anita Loos
C. John Steinbeck D. Tennessee Williams

832 Where was Captain Cook killed?
A. Jamaica B. Hawaii C. Mexico D. Tasmania

833 In which African country is Timbuctu?
A. Somalia B. Nyasaland C. Zimbabwe D. Mali

834 Where were the world's first traffic lights situated?
A. Outside the Houses of Parliament in Westminster, London
B. In Times Square, New York.
C. On Capitol Hill, Washington DC
D. At the junction of London's Oxford Street and Regent Street

835 Which British conductor once halted an orchestral rehearsal at the half-way stage, or thereabouts, organised a large TV to be brought onto the podium and settled down to watch the Cup Final?
A. Sir Malcolm Sargent B. Sir Colin Davis
C. Sir Thomas Beecham D. Sir Adrian Boult

836 By what nickname did Ronald Reagan call his first wife, actress Jane Wyman?
A. Her Nibs B. Peter Pan
C. Button Nose D. Jingle Belle

837 Of what is ichthyology the study?
A. Fish B. Birds C. Dinosaurs D. Fossils

838 How many Lonsdale belts has Henry Cooper won outright?
A. 1 B. 2 C. 3 D. 4

839 What was Count Basie's real first name?
A. Frederick B. Charles C. William D. Alan

840 Who won the 1984 Open Golf Championship at St Andrews?
A. Nick Faldo B. Severiano Ballesteros
C. Tom Watson D. Tom Weiskopf

841 Some 85 million people share the world's most common surname. What is it?
A. Smith B. Johnson C. Muller D. Chang

842 Who was the commander of the Israeli Army during the Six-Day War?
A. David Ben Gurion B. Moshe Dayan
C. David 'Mickey' Marcus D. Menachem Begin

843 The great pianist Claudio Arrau began his concert career at the age of 5. From which country did he come?
A. Spain B. USA C. France D. Chile

844 What is the chemical symbol for lead?
A. Pb B. Ld C. Lsd D. N1

845 Which American President was born on the same day as Charles Darwin, February 12, 1809?
A. Ulysses S Grant B. Abraham Lincoln
C. Grover Cleveland D. John Adams

846 Which is the lightest gas?
A. Oxygen B. Hydrogen C. Nitrogen D. Neon

ANSWERS pages 128–129: 831–A. 832–B. 833–D. 834–A. 835–C. 836–C. 837–A. 838–C. 839–C. 840–B. 841–D. 842–B. 843–D. 844–A. 845–B. 846–B.

---

847 William Cory, an assistant master at Eton, wrote the words to which well known song or hymn?
A. Rule Britannia B. The Eton Boating Song
C. Jerusalem D. Onward Christian Soldiers

848 The Gulf of Bothnia separates which two countries?
A. Sweden and Denmark B. USA and USSR (off Alaska)
C. Sweden and Finland D. Iceland and Greenland

849 Who was Argentina's top goal scorer in the 1978 World Cup, which they won?
A. Osvaldo Ardilles B. Ricardo Villas
C. Mario Kempes D. Pedro-Paulo Assumpçao

850 What was the value of the prize awarded to Charles Lindbergh for flying solo across the Atlantic?
A. 10 000 dollars B. 15 000 dollars
C. 25 000 dollars D. 50 000 dollars

851 Which Malayan style dress was popularised by Dorothy Lamour?
A. Dirndl B. Sarong C. Sari D. Cummerbund

852 In the main, what do the Milton Bradley company manufacture?
A. Musical instruments B. Carpets
C. Games D. Woolly jumpers

853 Which surname is most used by unmarried couples posing as married?
A. Brown B. Smith C. Jones D. Green

854 What is, or was, Kala Nag?
A. A snake B. A horse C. A bear D. An elephant

855 By what name is a cross between a grapefruit and a tangerine known?
A. Satsuma B. Nectarine C. Ugli D. Damson

856 The First Earl of Iveagh bequeathed which London house with its fabulous collection of paintings to the nation?
A. Somerset House B. Kenwood House
C. Apsley House D. Mansion House

857 Lemurs, the most primitive form of primates are mostly confined to which island or island group?
A. Madagascar B. Tasmania
C. Philippines D. Puerto Rica

858 Who, in the Bible, was renowned for his great patience?
A. Jesus B. Job C. Joshua D. Jeremiah

859 With whom was Sir Thomas More's head buried?
A. Sir Thomas More
B. His daughter
C. It was never buried but fell into the Thames from London Bridge where it was being exhibited, after he had been beheaded
D. It was never buried, but stuffed and placed in a museum, from which it was stolen and has never been seen to this day

860 Richard III was the last English King of which house?
A. Saxe-Coburg B. Tudor
C. Plantagenet D. Windsor

861 Where did Churchill and Roosevelt meet in 1943?
A. Chicago B. Checkers C. Casablanca D. Cardiff

ANSWERS pages 130–131: 847–B. 848–C. 849–C. 850–C. 851–B. 852–C. 853–B. 854–D. 855–C. 856–B. 857–A. 858–B. 859–B. 860–C. 861–C.

---

862 According to the Old Testament, which trees did Solomon use to build the Temple?
A. Oaks B. Mountain Ash
C. Cedars of Lebanon D. Olive

863 In which year did the GLC come into being?
A. 1945 B. 1955 C. 1965 D. 1975

864 Which country did Haile Selassie rule until 1974?
A. Pakistan B. Ethiopia
C. Saudi Arabia D. Afghanistan

865 In which county is Milton Keynes?
A. Bedfordshire B. Northamptonshire
C. Buckinghamshire D. Hertfordshire

866 What was Kate Greenaway's artistic speciality?
A. Sculpture B. Posters
C. Illustrations for children's books D. Ancient maps

867 What is the maximum driving speed in the USA?
A. 55 mph B. 65 mph C. 75 mph D. 85 mph

868 Queen Anne outlived all her children. How many did she have?
A. 5 B. 9 C. 13 D. 17

869 In which of London's parks is Rotten Row?
A. Regents Park B. St James's Park
C. Hyde Park D. Victoria Park

870 Who wrote 'The Skin Game'?
A. John Galsworthy
B. Jean Harlow
C. Frederick Forsyth
D. Marilyn Monroe (with assistance)

871 'Your Song' was the first record of which singer to make the British charts?
A. Tommy Steele B. Frank Sinatra
C. Gilbert O'Sullivan D. Elton John

872 Tchaikovsky's opera 'Eugene Onegin' was based on the work of which writer?
A. Shakespeare B. Chaucer
C. Dostoevsky D. Pushkin

873 By what name is the blues singer and composer McKinley Morganfield better known?
A. Muddy Waters B. Dizzy Gillespie
C. Billie Holliday D. Hairy Hands

874 What was the original name of the Old Vic theatre in London?
A. Globe B. Royal Coburg
C. Duchess D. Royal George

875 Who was assassinated in 1865 in Ford's Theatre?
A. Doc Holliday B. Billy the Kid
C. Abraham Lincoln D. John L Sullivan

876 Which British newspaper in 1972 wrote, 'One feels that Uganda cannot afford General Amin's warm hearted generosity'?
A. Daily Express B. Observer
C. The Times D. The Sun

ANSWERS pages 132–133: 862–C. 863–C. 864–B. 865–C. 866–C. 867–A. 868–D. 869–C. 870–A. 871–D. 872–D. 873–A. 874–B. 875–C. 876–C.

---

877 Which comedian was known as The Prime Minister of Mirth?
A. Max Wall B. George Robey
C. Harry Champion D. George Formby

878 Which was the first city to host the summer Olympic Games three times?
A. London
B. Paris
C. Stockholm
D. No city has hosted the Olympic Games three times

879 During World War Two, for what did WLA stand?
A. Women's Liberation Army B. Women's Land Army
C. West London Artillery D. Wheeled Land Army

880 Who, or what, was, or is Mons Meg?
A. A notorious female spy
B. A well authenticated vision of an angel, seen by thousands during the 1914 –1918 war
C. A blues singer from St Louis
D. A huge medieval cannon, based at Edinburgh castle

881 What was the first word that Anne Sullivan taught deaf and dumb Helen Keller to say?
A. Yes B. No C. It D. Please

882 What follows red in the traffic lights cycle?
A. Red and amber B. Green
C. Amber D. Amber and green

883 General 'Stonewall' Jackson's last words, 'Across the river and into the trees', were used as the title of a book. By which author?
A. John Steinbeck B. James Michener
C. Jack London D. Ernest Hemingway

884 Welwyn Garden City is in which English county?
A. Northamptonshire B. Hertfordshire
C. Bedfordshire D. Buckinghamshire

885 Who comperes 'The Late, Late Breakfast Show'?
A. Jeremy Beadle B. Mike Reid
C. Noel Edmonds D. Keith Chegwin

886 Who preceded John Adams as President of the USA?
A. Abraham Lincoln B. Theodore Roosevelt
C. Calvin Coolidge D. George Washington

887 What was the sequel to 'Gentlemen Prefer Blondes'?
A. 'Gentlemen Marry Brunettes'
B. 'Gentlemen Date Redheads'
C. 'Gentlemen Prefer Gentlemen'
D. 'Gentlemen Marry Blondes'

888 Which of the following is the musical term for 'very loudly'?
A. Allegro B. Con Brio C. Fortissimo D. Dulce

889 What is the motto of the Boy Scout and Girl Guide movements?
A. Always Ready to Lend a Hand
B. Be Prepared
C. At Your Service
D. Do unto Others as You Would Have Done unto Yourself

890 Of which country is Copenhagen the capital?
A. Denmark B. Sweden C. Finland D. Iceland

ANSWERS pages 134–135: 877–B. 878–D. 879–B. 880–D. 881–C. 882–A. 883–D. 884–B. 885–C. 886–D. 887–A. 888–C. 889–B. 890–A.

---

891 'March On, March On' is the national anthem of which country?
A. Canada B. Greece
C. India D. The People's Republic of China

892 What was John Larson's invention of 1921?
A. Windscreen wipers B. Artificial silk
C. Pneumatic tyres D. The lie detector

893 How many miles is the estimated circumference of Saturn's rings?
A. 50 000 miles B. 100 000 miles
C. 500 000 miles D. 1 000 000 miles

894 Dr Edward Jenner saved millions of lives by developing a vaccine against which disease?
A. Polio B. Smallpox
C. Bubonic Plague D. Tuberculosis

895 DDT was first invented in 1874. When was it first used as a pesticide?
A. 1899 B. 1919 C. 1939 D. 1959

896 Which was rock and roll's biggest single hit?
A. 'Peggy Sue' B. 'Rock Around the Clock'
C. ''Till I Kissed Her' D. 'Heartbreak Hotel'

897 What is British Honduras now called?
A. Belize B. Tunisia C. Niger D. Mauritania

898 In which year was the Magna Carta sealed?
A. 1066 B. 1125 C. 1215 D. 1601

899 In which county is Stonehenge?
A. Dorset B. Wiltshire
C. Hampshire D. Buckinghamshire

900 What is a roncador?
A. An American fish
B. An assistant at a bull fight
C. A trade name for the first electric razor
D. A curiously flattened Irish toadstool

901 In which year did Constantinople become Instanbul?
A. 1919 B. 1930 C. 1946 D. 1956

902 What was Buddy Holly's original back-up band called?
A. The Belmonts B. The Crickets
C. The Teenagers D. The Supremos

903 What did Robert Gibbon Johnson eat in 1820 that frightened people, but when he didn't die, they found them to be nutritious, not poisonous?
A. Potatoes B. Tomatoes
C. Pomegranates D. Green peppers

904 How many loaves did Jesus need to feed the 5000?
A. 5 B. 50 C. 500 D. 5 000

905 Which US President married Jacqueline Bouvier?
A. Franklin D Roosevelt B. Richard M Nixon
C. Lyndon B Johnson D. John F Kennedy

906 The word 'robot' is based on the Czech and Russian word of what meaning?
A. Work B. Drive C. Mechanic D. Automate

ANSWERS pages 136–137: 891–D. 892–D. 893–C. 894–B. 895–C. 896–B. 897–A. 898–C. 899–B. 900–A. 901–B. 902–B. 903–B. 904–A. 905–D. 906–A.

---

907 In 1928, Thornton Wilder won a Pulitzer Prize for a novel featuring a bridge. Which bridge?
A. Brooklyn Bridge B. London Bridge
C. Tallahatchie Bridge D. The Bridge of San Luis Rey

908 Who wrote and had a hit with 'Diana'?
A. Paul Anka B. Chuck Berry
C. Dion D. Buddy Holly

909 Which is the largest planet in the solar system?
A. Uranus B. Pluto C. Jupiter D. Saturn

910 Father Charles Goes Down And Ends Battle is the mnemonic for what?
A. The order of the sharps in musical key signatures
B. The Saxon Kings of England
C. The Presidents of the United States this century, up to World War Two.
D. The locations of the first 7 Winter Olympic Games

911 Who was Emperor of Rome when Jesus Christ was born?
A. Julius Caesar B. Augustus Caesar
C. Nero D. Claudius

912 In God We Trust is the motto of the USA. In which year was it adopted?
A. 1836 B. 1896 C. 1936 D. 1956

913 Which country had the first woman head of government?
A. Ceylon B. Great Britain C. India D. Israel

914 What was the family name of the last of the Russian Czars?
A. Ivanov B. Ulanov C. Petrov D. Romanov

915 Which composer wrote the three 'Leonora' overtures?
A. Bach B. Beethoven C. Brahms D. Bizet

916 Jean Baptiste Tavernier gave what present to King Louis XIV of France, the Sun King?
A. The Star of India B. The Hope Diamond
C. The Palace of Versailles D. The Eiffel Tower

917 Who played a garage attendant in Chris Petit's film, 'Radio On'?
A. Boy George B. Marilyn
C. Sting D. Art Garfunkel

918 What did Cassius Clay throw into the Ohio River in a fit of frustration?
A. His boxing gloves B. His Olympic Gold Medal
C. All the clothes that he was wearing D. His car

919 In which modern country is the site of ancient city of Carthage?
A. Mali B. Tanzania C. Tunisia D. Zimbabwe

920 In which century was (will be!) Buck Rogers?
A. 21st B. 23rd C. 25th D. 27th

921 Who starred in the 1955 musical film 'Guys and Dolls'?
A. Boris Karloff B. Spencer Tracy
C. Clint Eastwood D. Marlon Brando

ANSWERS pages 138–139: 907–D. 908–A. 909–C. 910–A. 911–B. 912–D. 913–A.(Now Sri Lanka) 914–D. 915–B. 916–B. 917–C. 918–B. 919–B. 920–C. 921–D.

---

922 Between which two US states does the Mason-Dixon Line pass?
A. North Carolina and South Carolina
B. Connecticut and New York
C. Virginia and Washington
D. Pennsylvania and Maryland

923 'The Mystery of Edwin Drood' was which writer's last work – in fact unfinished at his death?
A. Oscar Wilde B. Jonathan Swift
C. Charles Dickens D. Lewis Carroll

924 Was Sir Iain Moncreiff of that Ilk . . .?
A. A P G Wodehouse character
B. An Anthony Trollope character
C. A Sir Walter Scott character
D. A real person

925 What is loblolly?
A. A thick gruel B. Sheep's medicine
C. A lout D. The name for various American pines

926 Who was the Queen of Tonga from 1918 – 1968?
A. Queen Nefertiti B. Queen Maud
C. Queen Salote D. Queen Fatima

927 Which country is the world's largest producer of diamonds, gold and platinum?
A. Sri Lanka B. Mexico
C. South Africa D. Russia

928 What was August von Wasserman's claim to fame?
A. He invented the Bouncing Bomb
B. He perfected a test which detects syphilis in the blood
C. He discovered radioactivity
D. He was the uncle of Albert Einstein

929 Who wrote 'The Caine Mutiny?'
A. John Steinbeck B. Frederick Forsyth
C. James Michener D. Herman Wouk

930 What names do the H G represent in Mr Wells's name?
A. Herbert George B. Herbert Graham
C. Harvey George D. Harvey Graham

931 What is Cecil B DeMille's middle name?
A. Basil B. Bertram C. Boris D. Blount

932 Pirate Edward Teach was better known by what name?
A. Captain Kidd B. Blackbeard
C. Henry Morgan D. Captain Hook

933 Which outlaw was shot dead in El Paso on August 19, 1895?
A. Jesse James B. Butch Cassidy
C. John Wesley Hardin D. Sam Starr

934 Why were the Nazis particularly prone to varicose veins?
A. Because of the cut of their uniforms
B. From doing the goose step
C. Because their jackboots were too tight
D. Standing for hours at Nuremberg rallies

935 What was Malawi called before 1964?
A. Basutoland B. Nyasaland
C. Dutch New Guinea D. The Ivory Coast

ANSWERS pages 140–141: 922–D. 923–C. 924–D. 925–A bonus: loblolly is all of these. 926–C. 927–C. 928–B. 929–D. 930–A. 931–D. 932–B. 933–C. 934–B. 935–B.

---

936 What colour is the Queen's blotting paper?
A. Blue B. Red C. White D. Black

937 What did slot machines first dispense?
A. Bullseyes B. Holy water in ancient temples
C. Candles for worship D. Hair oil

938 What was the main reason for Queen Elizabeth I possessing nearly 100 wigs?
A. Sheer vanity
B. So that she didn't have to wash her hair too often
C. Because it was the norm
D. Because she was bald

939 Of what offence was George Smith the first to be convicted in Britain in 1897?
A. Drunken driving
B. Living off the earnings of prostitutes
C. Kidnapping young ladies for Eastern harems
D. Indecent exposure

940 Madame La Bresse of France left some extraordinary bequests in her will. Which of these were included?
A. Money to buy bootees for the stray dogs of Paris
B. A home for fallen women
C. A shop to sell food at half the going rate to the deserving poor
D. Money to provide clothes for snowmen

941 For what was Stenson Cooke noted?

A. He was the AA secretary who introduced the star ratings for hotels
B. He invented the barometer
C. He was an American contender for the World Chess Championship in the 1880s
D. He was the first zoologist to breed duck-billed platypuses in captivity

942 When Kal-El came to Earth, what name was he/she given?
A. Peter Parker B. Clarke Kent
C. Diana Prince D. Billy Batson

943 Which superhero's other identity is Billy Batson?
A. Superman B. Batman
C. Spiderman D. Captain Marvel

944 What did Peter Henlein invent in 1509?
A. The pocket watch B. The sextant
C. Chrome D. Golf

945 Who was William Howard Russell?
A. The Times foreign correspondent who covered the Crimean War
B. A celebrated horticulturist who specialised in lupins
C. Captain Cook's navigator
D. The Sixth Earl of Scarborough, famous for the old follies that he built around the countryside

946 As what were tomatoes originally known?
A. Love apples B. Red plums
C. Comforters D. Grand cherries

947 Which composer is associated with drunkenness?
A. Bach B. Beethoven C. Brahms D. Bizet

948 Of what is a xenophobe afraid?
A. Foreigners B. The dark C. Number 13 D. Work

ANSWERS pages 142–143: 936–D. 937–B. 938–D. 939–A. 940–D. 941–A. 942–B. 943–D. 944–A. 945–A. 946–A. 947–C. 948–A.

---

949 What is Aujeszy's disease?
A. A disease of pigs
B. A problem with 2-8 week old canaries
C. Another name for Parkinson's disease
D. A psychological complaint shared by 12-14 year old boys and 14-16 year old girls

950 In Greek mythology, which nymph changed into a spring to escape the amorous advances of the river god Alpheus?
A. Ariadne B. Anemone C. Arethusa D. Diana

951 Of what is triskaidekaphobia the fear?
A. Octopuses B. The dark C. Number 13 D. Work

952 How much did America pay Russia for Alaska in 1862?
A. 7 million dollars
B. 10 million dollars
C. 70 million dollars
D. 100 million dollars

953 In which year were women over 21 first permitted to vote in England?
A. 1919 B. 1921 C. 1928 D. 1931

954 What do Poles spend?
A. Zloty B. Dinar C. Peseta D. Zepel

955 What article of clothing was named after the Earl who led the charge of the Light Brigade?
A. Balaclava B. Cardigan
C. Wellington D. Macintosh

956 What is the brightly-coloured, loose dress worn by the women of Hawaii called?
A. A muumuu B. A kaakaa
C. A floofloo D. A chaachaa

957 In which city is there a street called The Shambles?
A. Leicester B. York C. Canterbury D. Coventry

958 Who first used the word 'dwindle'?
A. Francis Bacon B. William Shakespeare
C. Geoffrey Chaucer D. John Donne

959 Is a funambulist a . . .?
A. Trick cyclist B. Tightrope walker
C. Merry-go-round operator D. Sleepwalker

960 What was Leonard Rossiter's last film called?
A. 'Rising Damp' B. 'Water'
C. 'Cinzano Express' D. 'Marry Me, Miss Jones'

961 Who were the first people to wear wedding rings?
A. The Greeks B. The Romans
C. The American Indians D. The Egyptians

962 For what offence was Al Capone jailed?
A. Murder B. Bootlegging
C. Extortion D. Tax evasion

963 Who is the patron saint of pawnbrokers?
A. St Nicholas B. St Crispin
C. St Bernard D. St Augustine

964 Who invented scissors?
A. Michelangelo B. Henry VIII
C. Marco Polo D. Leonardo da Vinci

ANSWERS pages 144–145: 949–A. 950–C. 951–C. 952–A. 953–C. 954–A. 955–B. 956–A. 957–B. 958–B. 959–B. 960–B. 961–D. 962–D. 963–A. 964–D.

---

965 Which British Prime Minister resigned after the Suez Canal zone occupation controversy?
A. Winston Churchill B. Anthony Eden
C. Harold Macmillan D. James Callaghan

966 Trichology is the branch of medicine associated with . . .?
A. Fingers and toes B. Skin C. Hair D. Kidneys

967 Who was the last person kept in the Tower of London as a prisoner?
A. Mary, Queen of Scots B. Charles I
C. Lord Haw Haw D. Rudolf Hess

968 Whose mistress described him as 'mad, bad and dangerous to know'?
A. Nelson's B. Napoleon's
C. Lord Byron's D. Hitler's

969 Which American state is nicknamed 'Show Me State' and has Jefferson City as its capital?
A. Montana B. Nebraska C. Florida D. Missouri

970 Which American state is nicknamed 'Lone Star State' and has Austin as its capital?
A. Indiana B. Montana C. Texas D. Michigan

971 How long did the *first* Oxford Dictionary take to compile?
A. 5 years B. 10 years C. 20 years D. 50 years

972 From what is lead in lead pencils made?
A. Lead B. Cupro-nickel C. Graphite D. Charcoal

973 Local, or state, prohibition had been around for some while, but when did it become *national* in the United States?
A. 1918 B. 1920 C. 1922 D. 1924

974 What are Hackled Caperers and Orange Quills?
A. Fishing flies B. Butterflies
C. Toadstools D. Mexican cacti

975 What fashion did Henry Frederick, Earl of Arundel, start?
A. Wearing braces to hold up trousers
B. Having more than one Christian name
C. Raising hats to ladies
D. Changing from regular clothes into more suitable sportswear

976 Which famous poet played in the very first Eton v Harrow cricket match?
A. Alfred Lord Tennyson
B. Lord Byron
C. Henry Wadsworth Longfellow
D. William Wordsworth

977 As whom is Selina Kyle better known?
A. Deep Throat B. Cat Woman
C. Wonder Woman D. The Sugar Plum Fairy

978 How many times the weight of an average man is an average elephant?
A. 7 B. 37 C. 70 D. 107

979 Which was the first of the rare metals to be discovered?
A. Uranium B. Platinum C. Gold D. Silver

980 What was ex-Prime Minister Harold Wilson's first name?
A. Harold B. John C. James D. Edward

ANSWERS pages 146–147: 965–B. 966–C. 967–D. 968–C. 969–D. 970–C. 971–C. 972–C. 973–B. 974–A. 975–B. 976–B. 977–B. 978–C. 979–C. 980–C.

---

981 What was the surname of the first Duke of Marlborough?
A. Marlborough B. Churchill
C. Wellington C. Disraeli

982 Do more people die in . . .?
A. January/February B. March/April
C. September/October D. November/December

983 When did it become law for cars to be fitted with speedometers?
A. 1907 B. 1917 C. 1927 D. 1937

984 What has been the official language of Afghanistan since 1936?
A. Afghanese B. Urdu C. Russian D. Pashto

985 Which famous Briton was made Duke of Bronte by the King of Naples?
A. Wellington B. Nelson
C. Marlborough D. Disraeli

986 Which national championship did R M Foulds win for the third time in 1977 in a time of 101 minutes 22 seconds?
A. Shearing 100 sheep
B. Keeping 1 pipe of tobacco alight
C. Knitting a 10 foot scarf
D. Swimming Lake Windermere

987 In Arthur Ransome's book 'Swallows and Amazons', what was the surname of John, Susan, Titty and Roger?

A. Blackett B. Walker C. Swallow D. Forest

988 Who said in 1951, 'There will soon be only 5 kings left – the kings of England, Diamonds, Hearts, Spades and Clubs'?
A. Ex-king Farouk of Egypt
B. Ex-king Umberto of Italy
C. Ex-king Peter of Yugoslavia
D. Ex-king Zog of Albania

989 Which actor recorded the only spoken record to reach number one in the British hit parade?
A. Windsor Davies B. Lee Marvin
C. Telly Savalas D. Jon Pertwee

990 What was the only number one record by Cliff Richard that he wrote himself?
A. 'The Young Ones' B. 'Bachelor Boy'
C. 'We Don't Talk Anymore' D. 'Living Doll'

991 Which number one hit record was originally recorded as 'It's Only Your Lover Returning', but had its title changed at the last minute?
A. 'Don't Give Up on Us'
B. 'Don't Stand so Close to Me'
C. 'Don't Go Breaking my Heart'
D. 'Don't Cry for Me, Argentina'

992 Which famous pop singer won an exhibition to the Royal Academy of Music at the age of 11?
A. Petula Clark B. Elton John
C. David Essex D. David Bowie

993 In Hawaii, what sort of food is lomi lomi?
A. Pre-chewed coconut B. Sun-fried eggs
C. Hand-massaged salmon D. Baked octopus tentacles

ANSWERS pages 148–149: 981–B. 982–A. 983–C. 984–D. 985–B. 986–B. 987–B. 988–A. 989–C. 990–B. 991–D. 992–B. 993–C.

---

994 A ribible was a very early type of what?
A. Violin B. Microscope
C. Tennis racquet D. Indoor lavatory

995 What were Friendship, Aurora, Sigma and Faith?
A. 4 horses that pulled the Queen's Coronation Coach
B. 4 of the first American space-craft
C. 4 types of chairs made by Chippendale
D. 4 British ships sunk at Trafalgar

996 What have you been doing if you have indulged in simony?
A. Employing your own children in your business
B. Obtaining a job through false references
C. Employing farm-workers on short contracts
D. Selling jobs in the Church of England

997 Which famous composer sang 'God Save the Emperor' as he was dying?
A. Handel B. Haydn C. Schubert D. Schumann

998 In which sport is the game ended when the referee shouts 'Smug'?
A. Eton wall game B. Tiddly-winks
C. Conkers D. Marbles

999 What is odontoglossia?
A. A literary term for an unfortunate error whilst talking
B. An exotic type of orchid
C. A variety of toothless lizard
D. The inability to understand foreign languages

1000 If a friend gave you a Midnight Mollie, what should you do with it?
A. Put it in your sea-shell collection
B. Plant it in your rose-garden
C. Drink it and ask for another cocktail
D. Keep it in a tank with other tropical fish

1001 Which famous character in children's books was created by Barbara Euphan Todd?
A. Paddington Bear B. Worzel Gummidge
C. Marmalade Atkins D. Rupert Bear

1002 According to the ancient Greeks, precious stones like sapphires were divided into male and female stones. What made the difference?
A. Male sapphires were bigger and heavier
B. Female sapphires were smooth and males were rough
C. Male sapphires were a darker colour
D. Females were dull and males sparkled

1003 What relation is Princess Anne's son Peter to Queen Victoria?
A. Great-great-grandson B. Great-great-great-grandson
C. Great-great-great-great-grandson
D. Great-great-great-great-great-grandson

1004 Where would you buy a pair of cross garnets?
A. At a jeweller's – they're semi-precious stones
B. At a pet shop – they're tropical birds
C. At a theatrical costumiers – they're patterned tights for men
D. At an ironmongers – they're special hinges

1005 During which war did British soldiers first begin to smoke cigarettes?
A. Napoleonic War B. Crimean War
C. Boer War D. American War of Independence

ANSWERS pages 150–151: 994–A. 995–B. 996–D. 997–B. 998–D. 999–B. 1000–D. 1001–B. 1002–C. 1003–C. 1004–D. 1005–B.

1006 Which playing card is known as 'the curse of Scotland'?
A. 7 of hearts B. 8 of spades
C. 9 of diamonds D. 10 of clubs

1007 If you became expert in tribology, what would you know a great deal about?
A. The ancient Roman legal system
B. How groups of natives behave
C. Why some surfaces are slippery
D. Artificial hands and arms

1008 How long does the light from the sun take to reach the earth?
A. 48 seconds B. 8 minutes
C. 51 minutes D. 3¼ hours

1009 Which song was Britain's entry in the 1980 Eurovision Song Contest, and finished third?
A. 'Mary Ann', by Black Lace
B. 'The Bad Old Days', by Coco
C. 'Love Enough for Two', by Prima Donna
D. 'I'm Never Giving Up', by Sweet Dreams

1010 At Christmas, 1978, what was the basic weekly rate of pension for a single OAP?
A. £15 B. £19.50 C. £22 D. £27.50

1011 What are a Long Red Surrey and a French Short Horn?
A. Carrots A. Beef cattle
C. Moths D. Bantam cocks

1012 Which of these English kings was still king when he died?
A. Edward II B. Richard II
C. Henry II D. James II

1013 At what approximate speed does a wind qualify to be called a gale?
A. 40 mph B. 50 mph C. 60 mph C. 70 mph

1014 In American criminal slang, what is a 'snowshoe'?
A. A man-hole cover B. A decoy car
C. A plain-clothes cop D. A counterfeit 10 dollar bill

1015 Who said in 1975, 'I don't believe all the stuff I say'?
A. Ronald Reagan B. Muhammad Ali
C. Margaret Thatcher D. Brian Clough

1016 Where would you be if you landed at Galileo Galilei Airport?
A. Lisbon B. Naples C. Pisa D. Barcelona

1017 What's the meaning of Abu el-Houl, the Arabic name for the Sphinx.
A. Woman of the Desert B. Lion of the Night
C. The Silent One D. Father of Fear

1018 Who would be most likely to do a Randolph and Rudolph?
A. Trampolinist B. Ice-skater
C. Wrestler D. Gymnast

1019 Drinking mugs are occasionally made of pewter, but from what is pewter made?
A. Lead and copper B. Lead and tin
C. Copper and tin D. Lead and zinc

1020 What sort of creature is a sulphur-bottom?
A. Monkey B. Pig C. Whale D. Goose

ANSWERS pages 152–153: 1006–C. 1007–C. 1008–B. 1009–C. 1010–B. 1011–A. 1012–C. 1013–A. 1014–C. 1015–B. 1016–C. 1017–D. 1018–A. 1019–B. 1020–C.

1021 When was slavery made illegal in Britain?
A. 1751 B. 1771 C. 1791 D. 1811

1022 What is a Ritcher-Rauzer?
A. An opening in a chess game
B. A shepherd dance from Bavaria
C. A breed of mountain boar
D. A German slang term for a cobbled road

1023 What's the only breed of dog mentioned in the Bible?
A. Spaniel B. Mastiff C. Greyhound D. Terrier

1024 Who played the central character of the bomb disposal man Brian Ash in the 1978 television series Danger UXB?
A. Edward Woodward B. Jeremy Irons
C. Anthony Andrews D. Simon Ward

1025 To an Australian, what is a wobbegong?
A. A lazy shark who waits for the fish to swim to it
B. An aborgine word for a trained wallaby
C. A racehorse that makes a habit of finishing last
D. A surfer who loses his surfboard in the sea

1026 What's the date carved on the huge stone book held by the Statue of Liberty?
A. July 4th, 1789 B. July 4th, 1776
C. July 4th, 1884 D. July 4th, 1865

1027 Which vitamin has a natural source in the rays of the sun?
A. A B. B C. C D. D

1028 In which country could a visiting white man be referred to by natives as a pakeha?
A. Tibet B. New Zealand C. Japan D. Tahiti

1029 Why do bees perform a complicated movement called a 'waggle-dance'?
A. To tell other bees where to find food
B. To warn off strange bees from another hive
C. To fluff out the hairs on their legs to collect more pollen
D. To teach young bees how to fly

1030 Which American singer's only pop record to make the British charts was 'Mr Bass Man', in 1963?
A. Al Cornet B. Johnny Cymbal
C. Hank Guitar D. Andy Piano

1031 What is Kotch?
A. A German ball game played on ice
B. A comedy film starring Walter Matthau
C. A Stock Exchange slang term for a total loss
D. A basketball term for a clumsy shot that misses

1032 What was the first American TV series to be broadcast in China?
A. 'Charlie's Angels' B. 'The Incredible Hulk'
C. 'The Waltons' D. 'The Man from Atlantis'

1033 What are the middle names of the champion jockey Willie Carson?
A. Baker Cook B. Hunter Fisher
C. Paynter Barber D. Duke Ellington

1034 Who would be the best person to treat a case of dengue?
A. A vet B. A dentist
C. A physician D. A psychiatrist

ANSWERS pages 154–155: 1021–D. 1022–A. 1023–C. 1024–C. 1025–A. 1026–C. 1027–D. 1028–B. 1029–A. 1030–B. 1031–B. 1032–D. 1033–B. 1034–C.

1035 To an ancient Persian, what was a parasang?
A. A long curved sword B. A silver beaker
C. A distance of 3 miles D. A square ornamental rug

1036 What happened to Dudley Wayne Kyzer of Alabama in 1981?
A. He was sentenced to 10 000 years in jail
B. He found 10 million dollars in the street
C. He ate 10 gallons of strawberry icecream in 8 hours, then died
D. He got married for the 30th time

1037 In American slang, what is an oofus?
A. A blundering person B. A punch in the stomach
C. A hard-boiled egg D. A sudden heat-wave

1038 What did the Frenchman Hippolyte Mege-Mouries invent in the 1860s?
A. Galoshes B. Margarine C. Periscope D. Tuba

1039 What sort of a creature is an opah?
A. A Chinese mountain cat
B. A globe-shaped Atlantic fish
C. A small South American deer
D. A Middle Eastern vulture

1040 What did Jerry Siegel and Joe Shuster create in 1938?
A. The first television quiz show, called 'Backchat'
B. Nylon stockings

C. The first trampoline
D. The 'Superman' comic strip

1041 Which game has variations called one old cat and two old cat?
A. Darts B. Baseball C. Dominoes D. Poker

1042 In which city is the world's largest synagogue?
A. Jerusalem B. Tel Aviv
C. New York D. Philadelphia

1043 What do Italians know as 'zuppa Inglese' or 'English soup'?
A. Trifle B. Semolina C. Yoghurt D. Tomato paste

1044 What port in SE India is on the Bay of Bengal?
A. Calcutta B. Madras C. Bengal D. Bengazi

1045 Can you name the stockade where gold miners fought the troops in 1854 in Australia?
A. Alamo B. Eureka C. Triumph D. Knox

1046 Princess Margaret is Chancellor of which University?
A. Keele B. Birmingham
C. Oxford D. Heriot-Watt

1047 1. Secreto. 2. El Gran Senor. 3. Mighty Flutter. Who or what are they?
A. Code names for SAS operations
B. The first three home in the 1984 Derby
C. The proposed names for a new range of cigars
D. The Royal Mint's 'in house' names for coins and banknotes that they produce for other countries

1048 Salyut space station was home for 238 consecutive days in 1984 to how many Soviet cosmonauts?
A. 2 B. 3 C. 4 D. 5

ANSWERS pages 156–157: 1035–C. 1036–A. 1037–A. 1038–B. 1039–B. 1040–D. 1041–B. 1042–C. 1043–A. 1044–B. 1045–B. 1046–A. 1047–B. 1048–B.

1049 The law decided that the cat was not Sonny. Was it . . .?
A. Felix B. Tibbikins of Harrogate
C. Sugarpuss Patapaws D. Marmaduke Gingerbits

1050 Seven feet was high jumped for the first time in 1956. By whom?
A. Dick Fosbury B. Jesse Owens
C. Charlie Dums D. Dwight Stones

1051 What does singer Luciano Pavorotti keep in his pocket for good luck, whenever he sings?
A. A rabbit's foot B. A bent nail
C. An airline ticket D. A copy of the music

1052 For which month is sapphire the birthstone?
A. September B. October
C. November D. December

1053 What was band leader Glenn Miller's instrument?
A. Piano B. Trumpet C. Trombone D. Saxophone

1054 What is the average body temperature of a dog?
A. 96°F B. 99°F C. 101°F D. 105°F

1055 What sport does Calvin Peete play?
A. Basketball B. Badminton C. Golf D. Cricket

1056 When were the Gallipoli landings?
A. 1873 B. 1901 C. 1915 D. 1943

1057 Who was the deputy leader of the Labour Party when Hugh Gaitskell died in 1963?

A. Harold Wilson B. George Brown
C. Aneurin Bevan D. Stafford Cripps

1058 Who succeeded Hugh Gaitskell as leader of the Labour Party after his death in 1963?
A. Harold Wilson B. George Brown
C. Aneurin Bevan D. Stafford Cripps

1059 Who played the part of Paul McCartney's grandfather in the film 'A Hard Day's Night'?
A. The late Arthur Lowe
B. The late Sidney James
C. The late John Le Mesurier
D. The late Wilfred Brambell

1060 Who is, or was, Ben Lexcen?
A. The first New Zealander to win an Olympic Gold Medal
B. The designer of the keel that contributed to Australia winning the America's Cup
C. The inventor of nylon
D. The last man to see a live dodo

1061 What is 500 in Roman Numerals?
A. V B. L C. D D. M

1062 In 1957 Tom Clay, a Buffalo radio disc jockey was fired after barricading himself in and playing which record repeatedly for 17 hours?
A. 'That'll Be the Day', by the Crickets
B. 'Love Me Do', by the Beatles
C. 'Tie Me Kangaroo Down, Sport', by Rolf Harris
D. 'The Twist', by Chubby Checker

1063 Buffalo Bill's real name was William F Cody. For what did the F stand?
A. Frank B. Fergus C. Frederick D. Fellowes

ANSWERS pages 158–159: 1049–D. 1050–C. 1051–B. 1052–A. 1053–C. 1054–C. 1055–C. 1056–C. 1057–B. 1058–A. 1059–D. 1060–B. 1061–C. 1062–A. 1063–C.

1064 Who bought the Dorchester Hotel, London, in January 1985?
A. 'Tiny' Rowland B. Harold S Vanderbilt III
C. Robert Maxwell D. The Sultan of Brunei

1065 Which robot was the pal of spaceman Buck Rogers?
A. Sammi B. Tweeki C. Denri D. Doodi

1066 In which year did sweets and chocolates come off the ration after World War Two?
A. 1947 B. 1949 C. 1951 D. 1953

1067 In the long-running television series, which part was played in M*A*S*H by actor Gary Burgoff?
A. Corporal Klinger B. Father Mulcahy
C. Radar O'Reilly D. Colonel Potter

1068 Of what would you be guilty if you'd committed the crime of embracery?
A. Trying to bribe a jury
B. Stealing one of the Queen's swans
C. Trying to marry under the age of 16
D. Pretending to be a member of the armed forces

1069 In George Orwell's novel '1984', what did people refer to as a 'steamer'?
A. A rocket-bomb B. A prison cell
C. A trolley-bus D. A radio set

1070 Who created those furry creatures the Wombles, whose home is Wimbledon Common?

A. Mike Batt B. Elisabeth Beresford
C. Michael Bond D. Bernard Cribbins

1071 What was the Christian name of Mr Simpson, to whom Wallis Simpson was married before she became Duchess of Windsor?
A. Algernon B. Ernest C. Vernon D. Wallace

1072 In what occupation would you be most likely to suffer from 'tooth squeeze'?
A. Wrestler B. Deep-sea diver
C. Glass-blower D. Wine-taster

1073 Of what are you frightened if you suffer from brontophobia?
A. Lizards B. Sudden shocks
C. Thunder D. Poverty

1074 In 1890, James Gibb patented an invention he called 'Gossima'. What do we call 'Gossima' today?
A. Taffeta B. Table tennis
C. Tracing paper D. Talcum powder

1075 Which city has won the 'Britain in Bloom' trophy for the most beautiful flowers 7 times in the last 25 years?
A. York B. Southampton C. Belfast D. Aberdeen

1076 Which king designed his own Coronation robes, but made them so heavy that he fainted from the heat during the service?
A. Richard III B. Henry VIII
B. Edward IV D. George IV

1077 Glass-blowers in the Bristol area used to eat 'wallfish', because they were said to be good for the lungs. What were 'wallfish'?
A. Snails B. Mice C. Frogs D. Fungi

ANSWERS pages 160–161: 1064–D. 1065–B. 1066–D. 1067–C. 1068–A. 1069–A. 1070–B. 1071–B. 1072–B. 1073–C. 1074–B. 1075–D. 1076–D. 1077–A.

1078 Which weekly paper founded in 1940 was known as The Soldier's Friend?
A. Blighty B. Reveille C. Titbits D. Weekend

1079 What does a cartophilist collect?
A. Cigarette cards B. Postcards
C. Maps D. Bookmarks

1080 To travel on motorways vehicles must be capable of reaching what minimum speed?
A. 15 mph B. 20 mph C. 25mph D. 30 mph

1081 On weather maps, the symbol for snow is a small star with six points. What's the symbol for hail?
A. Diamond B. Square C. Triangle D. Circle

1082 Musically, how many semi-quavers make up a dotted minim?
A. 4 B. 6 C. 8 D. 12

1083 How did an American banker from Baltimore called Charlie Fenwick made headlines in 1980?
A. He swam the English channel six times
B. He rode the winner of the Grand National
C. He became engaged to Elizabeth Taylor
D. He parachuted from the top of Blackpool Tower

1084 Who has been designated the patron saint of Ecology?
A. St Bernadette B. St Francis
C. St Angela D. St Theresa

1085 If you visited Sherlock Holmes's old address as 221B Baker Street today, what organisation would you find there?
A. The British Pigeon Racing Organisation
B. An Abbey National Building Society office
C. The Romanian Tourist Agency
D. A Ladbroke betting shop

1086 What is a Kent Cob?
A. Nut B. Horse C. Biscuit D. Apple

1087 About whom did super-promoter Mark McCormack say, 'I see it as my duty to keep him in the 90 per cent tax bracket'?
A. The Pope B. Pele
C. Billy Graham D. David Frost

1088 What was composer Ivor Novello's real surname?
A. Jones B. Parry C. Evans D. Davies

1089 In Victorian slang, what was a 'London particular'?
A. A volunteer policeman B. A pea-soup fog
C. A two-horse cab D. Specially strong brew of beer

1090 What was remarkable about the birth of Emilio Marcos Palma in January 1978?
A. He weighed 23 lb, the heaviest baby ever
B. He was born in Concorde in flight
C. He was the first baby born in the Antarctic
D. He was the first ever test-tube baby boy

1091 What did Sir Henry Cole, director of the Victoria and Albert Museum, invent in 1846?
A. Cole slaw B. Christmas cards
C. Corned beef D. The monocle

1092 How long did it take to build Nelson's column in London?
A. 7 months B. 20 months C. 6½ years D. 27 years

ANSWERS pages 162–163: 1078–B. 1079–A. 1080–C. 1081–C. 1082–D. 1083–B. 1084–B. 1085–B. 1086–A. 1087–A. 1088–D. 1089–B. 1090–C. 1091–B. 1092–D.

1093 Where in the British Isles did a £1 coin first go into circulation?
A. Eire in 1977 B. Isle of Man in 1978
C. Guernsey in 1979 D. Jersey in 1980

1094 Of the famous people whose pictures appear on the reverse of British banknotes, who lived the longest?
A. £5 note, Duke of Wellington
B. £10, Florence Nightingale
C. £20, William Shakespeare
D. £50, Christopher Wren

1095 Which English cathedral once had a spire 525 feet high, which blew down in 1548?
A. York Minster B. Old St Paul's
C. Lincoln Cathedral D. Wells Cathedral

1096 From which country was Italy's first space satellite, San Marco I, launched in 1964?
A. USA B. Australia C. Brazil D. Venezuela

1097 Which Film Festival gives Gold and Silver Bears as prizes?
A. Berne B. Cannes C. Venice D. Berlin

1098 What did Cardinal Hume, Penelope Keith and Torvill and Dean have in common in May 1984?
A. They were invited to the White House by President Reagan
B. It was announced they were turning vegetarians
C. They were given freedom of the City of London

D. They were names used for new varieties of roses

1099 What was the original working title for, 'Coronation Street'?
A. 'Coming and Going' B. 'Balaclava Row'
C. 'Neighbours' D. 'Florizel Street'

1100 In which year did the British first run regular matinee shows for children only?
A. 1919 B. 1928 C. 1936 D. 1947

1101 Which initials were used by the first Nazi stormtroopers, led by Ernst Roehm, until he was purged by Hitler?
A. SA B. SB C. SS D. SZ

1102 What is a narthex?
A. A North African antelope with curved horns
B. A kind of pike used by 17th-century soldiers
C. A partition in an early Christian church
D. A pain-killer derived from herring oil

1103 In what field did Burrhus Frederic Skinner become extremely well-known?
A. Studying the psychology of rats
B. Playing American pro basketball
C. Collecting English folk songs
D. Designing Sydney Harbour bridge

1104 What were excluded from the Chelsea Flower Show in 1983, but had their own show at Peterborough instead?
A. Garden gnomes B. Cacti
C. Artificial flowers D. Mechanical diggers and tractors

1105 Who was the only person that Kit Williams, the author of 'Masquerade', entrusted with the secret of where he had buried the Golden Hare he had made?
A. Magnus Magnusson B. Sir Robin Day
C. Bamber Gascoigne D. Sir Robert Mark

ANSWERS pages 164–165: 1093–B. 1094–D. 1095–C. 1096–A. 1097–D. 1098–D. 1099–D. 1100–B. 1101–A. 1102–C. 1103–A. 1104–A. 1105–C.

1106 Which Nobel Prize did Henry Taube win in 1983?
A. Chemistry B. Physics
C. Economics D. Medicine

1107 Who is the President of Britain's Girl Guides?
A. Princess Anne B. Duchess of Kent
C. Princess Margaret D. Lady Baden-Powell

1108 Of which country did Mr Turgut Ozal become Prime Minister in 1983?
A. Turkey B. Albania C. Morocco D. Afghanistan

1109 Which European country watches the lowest amount of television, an average of 9 hours per person per week?
A. Belgium B. Eire C. Norway D. Greece

1110 Which pop group's video of their record 'Under Cover Of The Night' was rejected by British television companies because it was too violent?
A. Wham B. Rolling Stones
C. Thompson Twins D. Echo and the Bunnymen

1111 When thieves stole 3 tons of gold worth £25 million from Heathrow Airport, how many ingots made up the haul?
A. 2 400 B. 6 800 C. 9 400 D. 16 100

1112 What was the original intended title for the long-running radio serial, 'The Archers'?
A. 'Little Twittington' B. 'Barwick Green'
C. 'Rainbow Farm' D. 'Turpin Common'

1113 Which Russian author was a political prisoner, and had been blindfolded to be shot by firing-squad when a last minute reprieve arrived?
A. Tolstoy B. Solzhenitsyn
C. Chekhov D. Dostoevsky

1114 Comedian and film director Woody Allen once missed the Oscar ceremony to play in a jazz group. Which instrument does he play?
A. Clarinet B. Saxophone C. Piano D. Vibraphone

1115 In which country have the Sendero Luminoso or Shining Path guerrillas been opposing President Terry's government?
A. Sri Lanka B. Kenya C. Peru D. Samoa

1116 In June 1983, the contents of stately home Godmersham Park, Kent, fetched high prices at auction because of the house's connection with which author?
A. Kipling B. Jane Austen
C. Dickens D. Virginia Woolf

1117 Under which London Bridge was Italian financier Roberto Calvi, nicknamed 'God's Banker' because of his connection with Vatican funds, found hanging in 1982?
A. Waterloo B. Chelsea C. Lambeth D. Blackfriars

1118 How many of the 210 songs that the Beatles recorded in the 1960s were performed in London's Abbey Road studios'?
A. 35 B. 121 C. 188 D. 204

1119 Before the 1983 British General Election, there were 23 women MPs. How many were there after the election, out of 270 female candidates?
A. 16 B. 23 C. 27 D. 41

ANSWERS pages 166–167: 1106–A. 1107–C. 1108–A. 1109–C. 1110–B. 1111–B. 1112–A. 1113–D. 1114–A. 1115–C. 1116–B. 1117–D. 1118–C. 1119–B.

1120 What's the official name of the statue of Eros in London's Piccadilly Circus?
A. The Piccadilly Monument
B. The Prince Regent Memorial
C. The Shaftesbury Memorial
D. London Statue 831 RB

1121 When Sir Harold Wilson became a peer in 1983, he took the title of Lord Wilson of where?
A. Huyton B. Rievaulx C. Easingwold D. Hoylake

1122 Since 1982 a police constable from Bootle called Bill Bird has become much in demand for personal appearances because of his striking resemblance – to whom?
A. The Pope B. Elvis Presley
C. Ronald Reagan D. Prince Charles

1123 Who, when chosen as a castaway on Desert Island Discs, wanted to take as an optional luxury a yellow Lamborghini to drive up and down the beach?
A. Joan Bakewell B. Penelope Keith
C. Wendy Craig D. Angela Rippon

1124 In the USA, what is known as 'the mother of Presidents'?
A. West Point Military Academy
B. Harvard Law School
C. The State of Virginia
D. Young Democrats Summer Camp

1125 Who was 'the last of the red-hot Mamas'?
A. Gracie Fields B. Tessie O'Shea

C. Mae West D. Sophie Tucker

1126 In which television quiz game was Sarah Tisdall (imprisoned in 1984 for leaking a secret document to The Guardian) once a contestant?
A. 'Odd One Out' B.'Ask The Family'
C. 'The Krypton Factor' D. 'Mastermind'

1127 Which of these women from Greek mythology was one of the nine Muses?
A. Euphrosyne B. Thalia C. Clotho D. Megaera

1128 The longest Wimbledon men's singles final came in 1954, when Ken Rosewall lost 11-13, 6-4, 2-6, 7-9. Who beat him?
A. Lew Hoad B. Tony Trabert
C. Jaroslav Drobny D. Alex Olmedo

1129 What do employees of Britain's MI5 call their organisation?
A. The office B. The company
C. The firm D. The centre

1130 What was Mrs Margaretha MacLeod's stage name?
A. Marie Lloyd B. Adelina Patti
C. Lily Langtry D. Mata Hari

1131 For what special purpose do Australian aborigine men use a language called Dyalnguy?
A. For religious ceremonies
B. To plan wars and hunting raids
C. To talk to their mothers-in-law
D. For reciting tribal folk tales

1132 In which country did rubber trees first grow?
A. Brazil B. Malaysia C. Kenya D. Sri Lanka

1133 What was the name of the designer of the Volkswagen car?
A. Porsche B. Daimler C. Benz D. Panhard

ANSWERS pages 168–169: 1120–C. 1121–B. 1122–A. 1123–A. 1124–C. 1125–D. 1126–B. 1127–B. 1128–C. 1129–A. 1130–D. 1131–C. 1132–A. 1133–A.

1134 Which famous composer was sacked as a choirboy for cutting off another choirboy's pigtail?
A. Mozart B. Haydn C. Rossini D. Wagner

1135 Which film was the inspiration for the television comedy series 'Happy Days', starring Henry Winkler as the Fonz?
A. 'That'll Be the Day' B. 'American Graffiti'
C. 'Getting Straight' D. 'The Last Picture Show'

1136 About audience reaction to which play did Peter O'Toole say, 'They didn't get the jokes. It's a very funny play'?
A. Waiting For Godot B. The Romans In Britain
C. St Joan D. Macbeth

1137 What's the only species of deer where both male and female have antlers?
A. Reindeer B. Elk C. Moose D. Musk deer

1138 What is Margaret Thatcher's favourite drink?
A. Sherry B. Whisky C. Gin D. Cointreau

1139 When did France finally abolish the use of the guillotine?
A. 1919 B. 1938 C. 1949 D. 1981

1140 Who said, 'Democracy is the form of government in which the free are rulers'?
A. Stalin B. Aristotle
C. Hitler D. The Ayatollah Khomeini

1141 What did the Cree Indians use instead of money?

A. Fish hooks B. Tobacco pipes
C. Arrow-heads D. Polished shells

1142 Who are or were Melanie Wilkes and Charles Hamilton?
A. American ice-skating champions in 1978
B. The hero and heroine of Agatha Christie's first novel
C. Two would-be assassins of President Richard Nixon
D. Characters from 'Gone with the Wind'

1143 When did Mildred and Patty Hill compose 'Happy Birthday To You'?
A. 1872 B. 1899 C. 1915 D. 1936

1144 According to scientists, which drink should you give to a drunk to help his hangover?
A. Coffee B. Tea C. Orange juice D. Milk

1145 Which film actress who wrote a book about beauty care said about herself, 'Oh, I'm ugly, ugly'?
A. Jane Fonda B. Sophia Loren
C. Raquel Welch D. Brigitte Bardot

1146 Who was Junko Tabei?
A. The earliest historian of the Japanese martial code, in 1321
B. The first woman to climb Mount Everest, in 1975
C. The pirate who raided Hawaii in 1857
D. The chief of the Zulu tribe from 1920 to 1932

1147 Feather duster and cut lips are terms used in which sport?
A. Wrestling B. Angling C. Trampolining D. Polo

1148 Where in Britain is there a rail system known as the Magic Roundabout, which has carriages called Clockwork Oranges?
A. Newcastle B. Aberystwyth
C. Glasgow D. Bournemouth

ANSWERS pages 170–171: 1134–B. 1135–B. 1136–D. 1137–A. 1138–B. 1139–D. 1140–B. 1141–B. 1142–D. 1143–D. 1144–C. 1145–C. 1146–B. 1147–B. 1148–C.

1149 In 1981, who was nicknamed 'Mogadon Man', though the nickname didn't stick?
A. Ronald Reagan B. Michael Heseltine
C. Michael Foot D. Geoffrey Howe

1150 Which famous pop group once played in an American club under the pseudonym of 'Blue Monday and the Cockroaches'?
A. Rolling Stones B. Culture Club
C. Police D. Blondie

1151 Which pop singer signed up with a cosmetics firm to sponsor a range of nail varnish and eye paints, called 'Man-scratchers' and 'Soul Reflections'?
A. Toyah B. Boy George
C. Marilyn D. Debbie Harry

1152 In 1981, which newsreader tried to push a bed up Ben Nevis, but didn't make it?
A. Anna Ford B. Kenneth Kendall
C. Martyn Lewis D. Reggic Bosanquet

1153 When he was playing Karpov for the world chess championship, how did Korchnoi think Karpov's seconds tried to help him unfairly?
A. By sending him suggested moves telepathically
B. By laser beams aimed at the board
C. By sending coded messages in yoghurt
D. By walking past the stage in morse code

1154 What did H C Beck design that millions of people use every year?
A. The map of the London Underground system
B. The sculpture of the Queen's head on current coins
C. The arrangements of the letters on a typewriter keyboard
D. The original British telephone kiosk

1155 In World War Two, who was Arthur Axmann?
A. The one-armed leader of the Hitler Youth
B. The one-legged American Secretary of Defence
C. The one-eyed Australian Deputy Prime Minister
D. Churchill's codename when he travelled to Egypt in 1941

1156 Who made his fortune by patenting a device for making sugar cubes?
A. Henry Tate B. Joseph Lyle
C. John McDade D. Robert Sweetman

1157 Which of these was *not* said by Virginia Wade, the 1977 Wimbledon singles champion?
A. 'I don't make friends with the girls I'm playing against. It would be too painful to beat them'
B. 'If the worst comes to the worst I can go out charring'
C. 'I've always been delighted to be a woman'
D. 'I don't really class myself as an athlete. I'm an entertainer'

1158 Which of these balls in sport is the heaviest?
A. Golf ball B. Lawn tennis ball
C. Squash ball D. Fives ball

1159 Which of these sports do experts calculate is most demanding for the person taking part?
A. Karate B. Basketball
C. Fencing D. Weightlifting

ANSWERS pages 172–173: 1149–D. 1150–A. 1151–A. 1152–D. 1153–C. 1154–A. 1155–A. 1156–A. 1157–D. 1158–B. 1159–B.

1160 By what name do we better know Agnes Gonxa Bojaxhin?
A. Golda Meir B. Victoria Principal
C. Mother Theresa of Calcutta D. Mrs Lech Walesa

1161 Who is really Lynn Stringer?
A. Pauline Collins B. Faith Brown
C. Olivia Newton John D. Marti Caine

1162 What is GMUND?
A. A small town in Austria's Leiser valley
B. A Czechoslovakian sausage
C. A Polish shipping company
D. The General Municipal Union of Needlers and Dyers

1163 For which of these activities can you *not* be awarded a Pulitzer Prize?
A. Music B. Poetry C. History D. Economics

1164 Which country was responsible for popularising the sport of pigeon racing?
A. Belgium B. Britain C. USA D. Poland

1165 Which boxer who later became World Heavyweight Champion was disqualified in the Olympic Games for 'not trying'?
A. Floyd Patterson B. Muhammad Ali
C. Ingemar Johansson D. Joe Frazier

1166 In which city was the art-rock band 10CC formed in 1972?
A. Glasgow B. Detroit

C. Manchester D. Los Angeles

1167 Who said in 1940, 'Hitler has missed the bus'?
A. Chamberlain B. Churchill
C. Roosevelt D. The Duke of Windsor

1168 In the top-class 100 metre sprint, at what point of the race do experts calculate the athlete reaches his fastest speed?
A. After 20 metres B. After 40 metres
C. After 60 metres D. After 80 metres

1169 What was produced by Henry D Perky in Denver, Colorado, in 1893?
A. The first book token
B. The first cone for ice cream
C. The first ready-to-eat breakfast cereal
D. The first petrol pump

1170 In 1866, which firm was the first to produce boxes of assorted chocolates in Britain?
A. Cadbury B. Fry C. Rowntree D. Terry

1171 When was the electric chair first used for a convicted murderer, the execution taking place at Auburn Prison, New York?
A. 1870 B. 1890 C. 1910 D. 1930

1172 What did J Fletcher-Dodd build at Caister-on-Sea, Norfolk, in 1906?
A. The first sea-plane
B. The first tandem motorcycle
C. The first holiday camp
D. The first purpose-built cinema

1173 A Luftbery and a Chandelle are moves in what?
A. Backgammon B. Gymnastics
C. Skating D. Aerobatics

ANSWERS pages 174–175: 1160–C. 1161–D. 1162–A. 1163–D. 1164–A. 1165–C. 1166–C. 1167–A. 1168–B. 1169–C. 1170–A. 1171–B. 1172–C. 1173–D.

1174 What did Prince Henry of Prussia invent in 1911?
A. A lavatory for an aeroplane
B. The first jukebox
C. The first petrol cigarette lighter
D. Windscreen wipers for cars

1175 Which pop group's first LP to get into the charts was 'My Generation'?
A. The Who B. The Kinks
C. The Rolling Stones D. Pink Floyd

1176 One of the Great Train Robbers, Charles Wilson, escaped from prison in 1964, and was recaptured four years later – where?
A. Brazil B. Melbourne C. Quebec D. Morocco

1177 Which city is nicknamed 'City of Bells'?
A. Florence B. Madrid
C. Strasbourg D. Copenhagen

1178 Who, in addition to other titles, is the Duke of Rothesay?
A. The Queen B. The Queen Mother
C. Prince Charles D. Duke of Edinburgh

1179 Which King was the son of the Black Prince?
A. Edward II B. Henry II
C. Richard II D. He had no son

1180 Which country once used knives and spades as money?
A. Ancient Egypt B. Zimbabwe C. Korea D. China

1181 Which instrument did jazz musician Charlie Mingus play?
A. Double bass B. Clarinet C. Piano D. Drums

1182 Which mythical beast, born from a cock's egg hatched by a toad, could kill by staring at you?
A. Gorgon B. Griffon C. Manatee D. Basilisk

1183 If you are liable to titubate, what do you do?
A. Stammer when excited B. Stagger when walking
C. Wake yourself up by snoring D. Stand on your head

1184 Which of these Indian cities is furthest south?
A. Madras B. Bombay C. Calcutta D. Hyderabad

1185 Which of these countries doesn't have a border on Lake Victoria?
A. Uganda B. Zambia C. Kenya D. Tanzania

1186 Who was the last player to be top-seeded for the men's singles at Wimbledon and lose in the first round?
A. Ilie Nastase in 1973 B. Arthur Ashe in 1976
C. Manuel Santana in 1967 D. Roy Emerson in 1966

1187 Which British newspaper advertised itself between 1935 and 1959 with the slogan 'Forward with the People'?
A. News of the World B. Daily Herald
C. The People D. Daily Mirror

1188 Which large shop opened in London in 1909 with the slogan, 'This Famous Store needs no Name on the Door', and for some time had no name advertised above?
A. Harrods B. Liberty
C. Selfridges D. Debenhams

1189 The catchphrase 'Nice one, Cyril!' was begun by an advertising campaign – for what?
A. Bread B. Beer C. Chocolate D. Baked beans

ANSWERS pages 176–177: 1174–D. 1175–A. 1176–C. 1177–C. 1178–C. 1179–C. 1180–D. 1181–A. 1182–D. 1183–B. 1184–A. 1185–B. 1186–C. 1187–D. 1188–C. 1189–A.

1190 In which Gilbert and Sullivan opera does Sir Ruthven Murgatroyd disguise himself as Robin Oakapple?
A. 'Iolanthe' B. 'Ruddigore'
C. 'Trial by Jury' D. 'Patience'

1191 Which pop group shot to the top of the British charts in May 1984 with 'The Reflex'?
A. Ultravox B. Wham
C. Status Quo D. Duran Duran

1192 Who sang the title song for the 1974 Bond film 'The Man With The Golden Gun'?
A. Lulu B. Shirley Bassey
C. Carly Simon D. Paul McCartney

1193 Which television personality began his career as an engineering apprentice in Glasgow?
A. Jimmy Saville B. Nicholas Parsons
C. Hughie Green D. Matthew Kelly

1194 Which of these shipping weather forecast areas is furthest north?
A. Rockall B. Hebrides C. Forties D. Bailey

1195 In Australian slang, what's a jackeroo?
A. A trainee cattleman B. A young wallaby
C. A recently shorn sheep D. A lazy, worthless person

1196 Which Hollywood film producer's biography was called 'Don't Say Yes Until I Finish Talking!'?

A. Sam Goldwyn B. Darryl F Zanuck
C. Cecil B de Mille D. Erich von Stroheim

1197 Which 20th-century author who had bad eyesight often wrote with his nose?
A. James Joyce B. Evelyn Waugh
C. Aldous Huxley D. Joseph Conrad

1198 What did Rudyard Kipling, who was a keen golfer, invent to help him play more often?
A. Red golf balls for playing in the snow
B. Wheels for his bag of clubs
C. Luminous golf balls for playing at dusk
D. A thin folding raincoat to keep in his bag of clubs

1199 What did the French poet Gerard de Nerval take for a walk at the end of a blue ribbon?
A. A white kitten B. A lobster
C. A cheetah D. A peacock

1200 Which famous playwright once joked that he'd like to be buried standing up, and is in fact buried like that in Westminster Abbey?
A. Sheridan B. Bernard Shaw
C. Ben Jonson D. Christopher Marlowe

1201 Which famous poet liked to give exploding cigars to critics?
A. W B Yeats B. Alfred, Lord Tennyson
C. Dylan Thomas D. T S Eliot

1202 What's the most popular sport in American nudist camps?
A. Basketball B. Volleyball
C. Leapfrog D. Badminton

1203 How many letters are there in the Bible?
A. About 500 000 B. About 1 500 000
C. About 3 500 000 D. About 5 000 000

ANSWERS pages 178–179: 1190–B. 1191–D. 1192–A. 1193–B. 1194–D. 1195–A. 1196–B. 1197–C. 1198–A. 1199–B. 1200–C. 1201–D. 1202–B. 1203–C.

1204 Why did the state of Indiana ban 'Robin Hood' from its schools in 1953?
- A. They disapproved of British stories and wanted American ones used
- B. It glorified an undemocratic class system
- C. Robbing the rich to give to the poor was said to be Communist
- D. It was immoral to have a priest (Friar Tuck) committing crimes

1205 Which invented word was introduced to the English language for a bet by James Daly, a Dublin Theatre manager?
A. Quiz B. Goggle C. Moron D. Smog

1206 Why did wealthy Eugene Scheifflin import starlings and sparrows (previously unknown in the USA) to New York in the 1890s and release them in Central Park?
- A. He wanted America to have all the birds mentioned in Shakespeare
- B. New York was suffering plagues of flies
- C. He liked the chirping sounds they made
- D. He was a keen bird-watcher but got seasick easily and wouldn't sail to Europe

1207 In 1935, which country was the first outside Britain to begin a regular high-definition television service?
A. Germany B. Italy C. USA D. France

1208 Of which country was Aurangzeb the Emperor from 1658 to 1707?

A. Mexico B. Brazii C. India D. Persia

1209 Who was the first television news presenter to stand for Parliament?
A. Robin Day B. Ludovic Kennedy
C. Christopher Chataway D. Austin Mitchell

1210 In 1981, who was the first female newscaster to sing on British television?
A. Jan Leeming B. Angela Rippon
C. Anna Ford D. Selina Scott

1211 Which actor said, 'Sometimes I think a whole generation of youngsters will know me only as the man who did the Polaroid commercials'?
A. Lord Olivier B. Sir John Gielgud
C. Sir Alec Guinness D. Sir Michael Hordern

1212 Which sporting event was the first to be televised in Britain, as an experiment, in 1931?
A. The Derby B. Wimbledon
C. The Boat Race D. Thc Cup Final

1213 Why did the Danish astronomer Tycho Brahe always carry a small box of glue?
A. In case his wig came off
B. In case his false nose came off
C. In case his wooden foot came apart
D. In case the lenses of his spectacles fell out

1214 Which French author drank at least fifty cups of coffee a day, so that caffeine poisoning helped to kill him?
A. Victor Hugo B. Stendhal C. Voltaire D. Balzac

1215 Which city was attacked in Operation Dracula in 1945?
A. Bucharest B. Rangoon C. Shangai D. Arnhem

ANSWERS pages 180–181: 1204–C. 1205–A. 1206–A. 1207–A. 1208–C. 1209–C. 1210–A. 1211–A. 1212–A. 1213–B. 1214–D. 1215–B.

1216 Which English author was known to drink 25 cups of tea at one sitting?
A. Charles Dickens B. Dr Johnson
C. Lord Byron D. William Blake

1217 Why is London's Piccadilly so called?
A. 'Dilly' was an 18th-century slang word for a prostitute
B. The area was once owned by Lord Pickard
C. After a card club called the Picquet
D. Ornamental collars called 'piccadills' were made there

1218 Which city has the highest murder rate per head of population?
A. Detroit B. Miami C. Cape Town D. Belfast

1219 Which country is the only one to have a national flag whose two sides are different?
A. Paraguay B. Ghana C. Vietnam D. Fiji

1220 In which country is the world's deepest known cave, called Atea Kananda?
A. Cambodia B. Nepal
C. Papua New Guinea D. Indonesia

1221 From which language does the word 'synagogue' come, originally meaning 'assembly'?
A. Latin B. Greek C. Hebrew D. Persian

1222 Travellers through desert areas during sandstorms can suffer nausea and severe headaches. Why?
A. The air is highly charged with electricity
B. Losing sight of the horizon affects the balance of the inner ear
C. Tiny particles of sand are absorbed by the sinuses
D. The skin becomes rapidly dehydrated and heated

1223 The largest iceberg ever sighted was the size of a European country – which one?
A. Vatican City B. Monaco
C. Luxembourg D. Belgium

1224 Which top English darts player has hinges tatooed on the inside of his elbows?
A. Dave Whitcombe B. Dave Lee
C. Mike Gregory D. Bobby George

1225 Psychiatrists at the University of Washington have calculated which events in your life cause you dangerous stress. Which of these is most stressful?
A. Moving house B. Retiring from work
C. Going on holiday D. Son or daughter leaving home

1226 Which James Bond film begins with a skier shooting over a cliff and falling several thousand feet before opening his parachute?
A 'The Spy Who Loved Me' B. 'Moonraker'
C. 'Live and Let Die' D. 'For Your Eyes Only'

1227 What was the name of the ginger cat who, with Warrant Officer Ripley, survived all attacks on the spaceship Nostromo in the 1979 film 'Alien'?
A. Smith B. Brett C. Jones D. Harvey

1228 When did Robin Hood first appear in a cinema film?
A. 1896 B. 1909 C. 1917 D. 1923

ANSWERS pages 182–183: 1216–B. 1217–D. 1218–C. 1219–A. 1220–C. 1221–B. 1222–A. 1223–D. 1224–B. 1225–B. 1226–A. 1227–C. 1228–B.

1229 Which of these films starring Cary Grant was *not* directed by Alfred Hitchcock?
A. 'Suspicion' B. 'Indiscreet'
C. 'Notorious' D. 'To Catch a Thief'

1230 What did the philosopher Wittgenstein provide in his rooms at Cambridge for his students to sit on?
A. Empty beer kegs B. Deckchairs
C. Shooting-sticks D. Hammocks

1231 What were first used by the film director D W Griffith for 'Intolerance' in 1916?
A. False eyelashes B. Stuntmen
C. Subtitles D. Flashbacks

1232 At which place of work were employees before World War One forbidden to wear moustaches, though only during working hours?
A. Harrods B. The Stock Exchange
C. The Bank of England D. The Ritz Hotel

1233 In which country do people begin their spring cleaning by smashing jugs against their front doors and shouting, 'Away with fleas and mice!'?
A. Russia B. Greece C. Turkey D. Portugal

1234 Which independent country apart from Britain uses the tune of 'God Save the Queen' for its national anthem?
A. Liechtenstein B. Sweden
C. Mexico D. Luxembourg

1235 What is Krung Thep?
A The Cambodian name for Vietnam
B. The Thai name for Bangkok
C. The Korean name for Japan
D. The Malaysian name for Singapore

1236 Which place became capital of its country only four years after being made a city?
A. Oslo B. Canberra C. Ottawa D. Bonn

1237 Who said, 'When I'm caught between two evils, I take the one I've never tried'?
A. Mae West B. Oscar Wilde
C. Dorothy Parker D. Noel Coward

1238 Which of these films starred Peter Sellers?
A. 'The Magic Box' B. 'The Magic Christian'
C. 'The Magic Face' D. 'The Magic Bow'

1239 Which of these actors *didn't* play Dracula in a film?
A. David Niven B. Peter Cushing
C. Christopher Lee D. Bela Lugosi

1240 Which of these actors has played both Frankenstein and Frankenstein's monster, though in different films?
A. Peter Cushing B. Basil Rathbone
C. Boris Karloff D. Christopher Lee

1241 If a friend gave you a Russian Blue, what would be the most appropriate thing to do?
A. Open a tin of cat food for it
B. Put it in a rabbit hutch
C. Stick it in a stamp album
D. Keep it in your pigeon loft

1242 To a farmer, what's a Red Ruby?
A. Radish B. Cow C. Chicken D. Carrot

ANSWERS pages 184–185: 1229–B. 1230–B. 1231–A. 1232–C. 1233–B. 1234–A. 1235–B. 1236–C. 1237–A. 1238–B. 1239–B. 1240–C. 1241–A. 1242–B.

1243 How many gold medals for swimming did Mark Spitz win in the Olympic Games in Mexico City?
A. 2 B. 5 C. 7 D. 9

1244 In which sport did Lorna Johnstone represent Britain in the 1972 Olympic Games, 5 days after reaching her 70th birthday?
A. Rowing, as a cox B. Dressage
C. Archery D. Rifle shooting

1245 Which University provided the team who won the first-ever University Challenge knockout tournament, back in 1964?
A. Leicester B. Sussex C. Durham D. St Andrews

1246 In 1940, what did the Germans call 'Moonlight Sonata'?
A. A plan to put agents into Ireland
B. An attack on Cairo from the desert
C. A bombing raid on Coventry
D. A plan for the invasion of Norway

1247 Which arm and which eye did Nelson lose in battle?
A. Left arm and left eye B. Left arm and right eye
C. Right arm and left eye D. Right arm and right eye

1248 Which well-known ballet has the sub-title 'The Girl with the Enamelled Eyes'?
A. 'La Fille Mal Gardée' B. 'Pineapple Poll'
C. 'Coppelia' D. 'Giselle'

1249 Who was Sherlock Holmes's housekeeper?

A. Mrs Hudson B. Mrs Bridges
C. Mrs Bellamy D. Mrs McTavish

1250 How many players make up a water-polo team?
A. 4 B. 5 C. 6 D. 7

1251 How many sides did the pre-decimal threepenny piece have?
A. 7 B. 8 C. 10 D. 12

1252 Which World War Two aeroplane was nicknamed 'the Stringbag'?
A. Gloster Gladiator B. Lancaster
C. Fairey Swordfish D. Hawker Hurricane

1253 Which cathedral city stands on the River Ure?
A. Chester B. Bath C. Winchester D. Ripon

1254 Which British rock group began as the New Yardbirds, formed by Jimmy Page?
A. Pink Floyd B. Led Zeppelin
C. Moody Blues D. Genesis

1255 Who were the first punk rock band to release a record in Britain?
A. The Damned B. The Sex Pistols
C. The Stranglers D. The Buzzcocks

1256 In which English city did Two-Tone Rock begin?
A. Liverpool B. Newcastle
C. Coventry D. Manchester

1257 What is a Fender Stratocaster?
A. Hang-glider B. Motorbike
C. Fishing rod D. Electric guitar

ANSWERS pages 186–187: 1243–A. 1244–B. 1245–A. 1246–C. 1247–D. 1248–C. 1249–A. 1250–D. 1251–D. 1252–C. 1253–D. 1254–B. 1255–A. 1256–C. 1257–D.

1258 In which American rock group, originally the Warlocks, was Ron 'Pigpen' McKerman the harmonica player?
A. The Eagles B. The Grateful Dead
C. Sly and the Family Stone D. Captain Beefheart

1259 Whose last words were said to be, 'I am dying as I have lived – beyond my means'?
A. Voltaire B. Lord Byron
C. Oscar Wilde D. Van-Gogh

1260 In Amsterdam it is illegal to re-roof your house unless you provide nesting-places for which birds?
A. Swifts B. Herons C. Storks D. Robins

1261 In the 19th century, who was known as 'the Sailor's Friend'?
A. Horatio Nelson B. Samuel Plimsoll
C. Samuel Cunard D. Robert Fulton

1262 On November 2nd, 1924, which British newspaper became the first to publish a crossword?
A. The Observer B. The Times
C. The Sunday Express D. The News Chronicle

1263 To what positions were George, Earl of Orkney, and John, Duke of Argyll, the first men to be appointed in 1736?
A. Royal gynaecologists
B. Field-marshals in the Army
C. Guardians of the Tower of London
D. Controllers of the King's Mails

1264 What did the Rev Jonathan Scobie, an American Baptist minister, invent in 1869?
A. A milking machine B. Luminous paint
C. The rickshaw D. Barbed wire

1265 Which Hollywood film star was the fastest draw, and could draw and fire a six-gun in a third of a second?
A. Clint Eastwood B. Jerry Lewis
C. Audie Murphy D. Sammy Davis, Jnr

1266 In 1941, Orson Welles was nominated four times for 'Citizen Kane', but won only one Oscar – which one?
A. Best Producer B. Best Director
C. Best Actor D. Best Writer

1267 Which film of the 1960s took most money at the box-office?
A. 'Mary Poppins' B. 'The Graduate'
C. 'Ben Hur' D. 'Thunderball'

1268 In which film did Greta Garbo say, several times, 'I vant to be alone'?
A. 'Anna Christie', 1930 B. 'Grand Hotel', 1932
C. 'Queen Christina', 1933 D. 'The Painted Veil', 1934

1269 Which film star believes that in a past life he was a railway worker in Africa in the 1860s who drank himself to death?
A. Clint Eastwood B. Roger Moore
C. Charles Bronson D. Sean Connery

ANSWERS pages 188–189: 1258–B. 1259–C. 1260–A. 1261–B. 1262–C. 1263–B. 1264–C. 1265–B. 1266–D. 1267–B. 1268–B. 1269–D.